Training Asians to Reach the World

Essays Honoring Everett and Evelyn McKinney
for 50 Years in Missions

Dave Johnson
EDITOR

WIPF & STOCK · Eugene, Oregon

Wipf and Stock Publishers
199 W 8th Ave, Suite 3
Eugene, OR 97401

Training Asians to Reach the World
Essays Honoring Everett and Evelyn McKinney for 50 Years in Missions
By Johnson, Dave
Copyright©2019 APTS Press
ISBN 13: 978-1-5326-8013-7
Publication date 2/21/2019
Previously published by APTS, 2019

TABLE OF CONTENTS

Foreword	i
Introduction *Dave Johnson*	1
Fulfilling a Vision: Reaching and Training in Many Nations *Dynnice Rosanny D. Engcoy*	5
Tell it To Your Children's Children *Kay Fountain*	21
Letting God's Life Form Our Life: Towards a Pentecostal Practice of Bible Reading *Monte Lee Rice*	35
Towards Becoming a Transformational Teacher: Teachers' Delivery Style Harmonizing with Students' Learning Style *Weldyn Houger*	59
How Cultural Anthropology Informs and Enhances Doing Theology and Theological Education in Asia *Dave Johnson*	81
Innovation in Christian Higher Education: The Case of the Oxford Centre for Mission Studies *Julie Ma*	99

Collaborative Partnerships in APTS 125
Yee Tham Wan

Appendix 1: Everett McKinney's Ministry Resume 133

Appendix 2: Evelyn McKinney's Ministry Resume 135

Contributors 137

FOREWORD

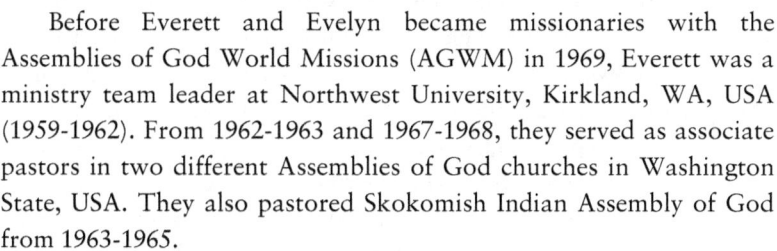

Everett and Evelyn McKinney have a great passion for God, ministry, and biblical education. Moreover, they are prayer warriors and have witnessed many miracles in their lives. Somewhere around 2000 my wife and I became acquainted with the McKinneys and immediately knew that this was a couple we needed to connect with often.

Before Everett and Evelyn became missionaries with the Assemblies of God World Missions (AGWM) in 1969, Everett was a ministry team leader at Northwest University, Kirkland, WA, USA (1959-1962). From 1962-1963 and 1967-1968, they served as associate pastors in two different Assemblies of God churches in Washington State, USA. They also pastored Skokomish Indian Assembly of God from 1963-1965.

Their first assignment, as appointed missionaries on the Philippine Field, was at Immanuel Bible Institute (1969-1975) where Everett served as president, business manager and faculty. Evelyn was the Academic Dean and a faculty member. From 1977 to 1984 Everett was the president of Far East Advanced School of Theology (FEAST and now Asia Pacific Theological Seminary - APTS) from 1977-1984; he also served as a faculty member at the institution. Evelyn was a faculty member and served as the Interim Academic Dean and Dean of Students for one year during their time at FEAST. Since 1987 to the present Everett and Evelyn have served as non-resident faculty at APTS.

They have been Bible school educational consultants for the Asia Pacific Education Office (APE0) since 1988. Evelyn serves as the secretary for the Teacher Development & Certification Commission (TDCC) under the Asia Pacific Theological Association (APTA). Both Everett and Evelyn have been a tremendous blessing and encouragement to the Asia Pacific Region Bible schools as well as those in other parts of the world. Their wisdom, years of educational experience and advice are greatly appreciated and applied in various Bible school contexts!

They have ministered in the Asia Pacific Region for 50 years and continue to do so. Everett and Evelyn have had a traveling teaching/preaching/seminary ministry since 1988. Within this time frame, they have ministered and taught in many places around the world (Continental Theological Seminary, Brussels, Belgium; Southern Asia Bible College, Bangalore, India; Evangel Theological Seminary, Kiev, Ukraine).

God's calling upon their lives has connected them with many church leaders and students. They walk in the Spirit, step out in faith and live their lives for the glory and honor of God. Students are very important to Everett and Evelyn. A few years ago they could have made the decision to retire from teaching, training and equipping students. But no! They kept going! And they continue to go around the world preparing students as laborers for the ripened harvest fields around the world. They continue to build strong relationships with their students and students love, respect and honor Everett and Evelyn.

Everett and Evelyn have a passion for the Word of God, equipping the students for ministry, and following the leading of the Holy Spirit. Both of them are sensitive to the voice of the LORD. They will stop what they are doing (even if it is in the classroom) and allow the Holy Spirit to have His way! They desire for the student to be people of the Word and to obediently follow the inspired Word. They are cognizant of the students' ministry environment. In addition to being equipped with the Word, they want the students to have a variety of teaching and preaching skills to be used in the students' ministry context. They will lead the students to be immersed in the power of the Holy Spirit and instruct the students to give precedence to the leading of the Spirit.

One last observation about this couple is their marriage. They have been married for more than 54 years. My wife and I have watched their marriage. They truly love each other! Has it been easy? No! Are there ups and downs in marriage and ministry? Yes! They strongly believe that when they exchanged their wedding vows, they were ready for whatever came their way; and they always had the LORD with them to guide their lives through difficult ways and decisions. They take each other's hands and look towards Christ Jesus from whence comes their help and strength. They have exemplified their marriage before hundreds of students, faculty, administrators and their colleagues. They are more in love with each other than ever before. They have a strong relationship with each other.

I can say with confidence that if there is one thing they desire from you, the reader, is that whatever God has put on your heart and in your mind, accept the call and direction of the LORD, be filled with the Word, and be empowered with Holy Spirit! When you obey and surrender to the command to go and make disciples, the Kingdom of God will grow!

PS: Everett and Evelyn are also expert taco makers!

Dr. Weldyn B. Houger

Everett and Evelyn McKinney

INTRODUCTION

Dave Johnson

A PTS Press is pleased to offer this volume as a small token of our love and respect for Everett and Evelyn McKinney. The Scriptures teach us that those who serve us well are worthy of double honor (I Timothy 5:17) and this is our effort to do just that. All of the scholars here are friends, colleagues or former students of the McKinneys and know them well. Each author, following the general theme of Training Asians to Reach the World writes within their specific area of interest.

Rose Engcoy opens this festschrift with a biological sketch of Everett and Evelyn McKinney. From their humble beginnings in rural America, God led them on an amazing journey that has taken them on an international teaching ministry in over 100 countries of the world.

They came into missions the traditional way by going to Bible school, after whcih they found and married one another and did a stint of pastoral ministry in America before arriving in the Philippines in 1969 to begin their missionary career.

For several years they led a Bible Institute in the central part of the Philippines. Then God called them to the Far East Advanced School of Theology in Manila, now known as the Asia Pacific Theological Seminary in Baguio City, Philippines. After a number of years there, the Spirit moved them into an international, itinerant teaching ministry in which they have continued to this day.

After Engcoy, the articles follow a gradual progression from the cradle to the PhD level. First, Kay Fountain reminds us that theological education begins in the home, not the seminary. The first teachers, then, are parents, not theological educators. Drawing on nine passages in the Old Testament and several in the New, she makes a compelling case for parental responsibility in spiritual matters. In looking at the situation in Asia after 25 years of involvement in missions there, she laments that so many Asians Christians do not appear to take this responsibility with the seriousness that they should.

Next, Monte Lee Rice delves into Pentecostal hermeneutics. His setting is not the classroom but the pew as he explores how ordinary Pentecostals read the Bible which, he contends, is somewhat different from the way that other Evangelicals examine Holy Writ. He then proposes to address these incongruities by composing a Pentecostalized form of the *Lectio Divina* (sacred reading). Beginning with an articulation of four qualitative distinctives of the way Pentecostals actually read the Bible, he points us in the direction that he thinks we should go.

Weldyn Houger takes us into the Bible school/seminary classroom to discuss the harmonization of the instructor's teaching style and the learning styles of the students. He contends that unless these are synchronized to a great degree, learning will be lessened. He then cites the works of multiple scholars that discuss the need, as well as the hows and whys, for this harmonization to take place.

Moving on to graduate and post-graduate level education, my contribution takes us to the nexus between theology and cultural anthropology, focusing on two of Paul's sermons in Acts. The first is to the Hellenized Jews in Pisidian Antioch in Acts 13:13-42 and the second is his message to the Athenian philosophers on Mar's Hill in Acts 17:16-34. Here, using the tools of cultural anthropology, I demonstrate the similarities and dissimilarities of the worldviews of the monotheistic Jews and the polytheistic Athenians, making application not only to Asian worldviews, but also how theological education can and must address these issues in modern Asian contexts.

Julie Ma then takes us to the post graduate level of studies, tracing the history of the Oxford Centre for Mission Studies in Oxford, United Kingdom. Rooting the history deep in the evangelical context, especially as it includes the unbiblical division between evangelism and social ministries, she demonstrates how the founding of the OCMS has contributed to healing this unnecessary division. At the same time, she demonstrates how rooting the Centre in England and following a European philosophy of education that allows for greater flexibility in content and management than its American counterpart has allowed the Centre to focus on missions research, especially in the area of wholistic missions in the Majority World, at the post graduate level. From wobbly beginnings in the 1980s, the Centre has emerged as a primary place of research in the 21st century and through its journal, *Transformation* and it's book publishing arm, *Regnum Books International,* has made a solid contribution to missiological research.

Finally, APTS President Tham Wan Yee takes us into the world of partnership in missions, especially in theological education. He contends that there are three broadly applied paradigms of partnership, Financier-Partner, Facilitator-Partner and Collaborator-Partner. He weighs the strengths and weaknesses of each and giving evidence as to which one he thinks is best.

We hope you enjoy our efforts to honor our dear friends. Any comments can be sent to us through our website, www.aptspress.org.

For the Glory of God,

Dave Johnson, DMiss
Editor

FULFILLING A VISION: REACHING AND TRAINING IN MANY NATIONS

Dynnice Rosanny D. Engcoy

Introduction[1]

Pastor, Teacher, Evangelist, Missionary, Bible School President, Seminary President, Academic Dean, Business Manager, Mentor, Pioneer Supporters – and the list goes on. In their 50 years of missions ministry, the McKinneys have mentored and trained workers now serving in over 100 countries.[2] But how did they start in this ministry? What challenges did they face? What has kept them going all these years? Most of all, what can we learn from their awesome legacy?

May this condensation of the spiritual heritage of these humble spiritual giants spur us on to also, by God's grace, fulfill our own God-given vision.

---

[1] Unless otherwise stated, information in this short biography comes from this writer's personal interviews with the McKinneys in Manila on March 27 and April 6, 2018.

[2] The McKinneys have ministries in Asia Pacific, Europe, Eurasia, and the Pacific Islands.

Where It All Began[3]

Everett

In an unpainted mountain cabin in Arkansas, with no electricity, no running water, 7 miles from the nearest paved road, a young 12-year-old boy was visited on several occasions by a Man through a vision. The Man told him, "I love you. I have a great plan for you." Then the Man showed him faces of people – red, brown, yellow, black, white. And He told the uncomprehending boy, "One day, my plan for you is that you will be training pastors and leaders and workers for the nations of the world." The young lad didn't know what to make of those visits nor could he see how things showed him could ever be possible.

It was not until he was seventeen years old when teen-age street evangelists witnessed to him that Everett finally came to know Christ in a personal way. Then, when he attended an Oral Roberts tent meeting, he accepted Christ as his Savior. He came to understand that God loved him so much that He sought him out in a mountain cabin years before he knew Him. And if God loved him so much that He sought him out, what about the people of the nations of the world that never heard the message yet? That so impacted Everett that he decided to go back and finish his high school then go on to Bible college, just so he could get the training necessary to fulfill God's plan in his life.

While in Northwest University, Everett did two summer mission trips in Mexico and Jamaica. He had to work full-time to be able to go to Bible college, so he completed the 4-year BTh course in 5 years.

Evelyn

Evelyn was born in the humble log cabin home of a logger who became a shoe repairman after he was miraculously healed following a terrible accident. Life was simple for her, but it was filled with many church activities.

---

[3]Information in this section comes from "Everett's Conversion, Call, and Preparation for Ministry" and "Evelyn's Conversion, Call, and Preparation for Ministry," articles sent by Everett McKinney to this writer on April 24, 2018.

Evelyn's parents loved missionaries and often invited them for dinner in their small home. As a young girl, she loved their stories and dreamed of becoming a missionary. When she went to Seattle Pacific University, she did a double major in Education and Missions. She then applied to be an Assemblies of God missionary. However, she was encouraged by the Assemblies of God World Missions (AGWM) to get some experience, so she taught in a public school and worked in a local church.

Everett met Evelyn when his Northwest University team ministered in her church. They were married after his 4th year and the summer in Jamaica. Evelyn continued to teach school while Everett finished Bible college, pastored, and also finished a BA in Education, all the while working toward AGWM appointment. Finally appointed as missionaries in 1968, they arrived in Manila harbor on a Norwegian freighter on September 12, 1969 and proceeded to Immanuel Bible Institute (IBI, now Immanuel Bible College, IBC) in Cebu City. Everett was appointed President in 1969 and Evelyn was Academic Dean until a national was appointed.

Challenges and Opportunities – Cebu Years

The McKinneys came to the Philippines knowing that life would be different. They often say that their greatest asset is knowing that they don't know. Learning to accept differences is important. They keep in focus that "different" is not better or worse – different is different! Their openness greatly helped them as they faced the challenges of their new mission field.

Both the McKinneys were fully involved with the people from the moment they arrived. Their philosophy of missions was to work closely with nationals. One proof of their closeness to the nationals was the fact that many locals called them *"Tatay"* and *"Nanay"* McKinney ("Dad" and "Mom" McKinney), terms of respect and endearment that Filipinos reserve for those who have established close relationships with them. The couple focused on ministering to the people, challenging them for missions, and helping them know what God was doing in different places around the world. To the pastors they asked, "What can we do to help you? How do you need help?"

Seeing such a great need for pastors and more churches, Everett travelled a lot doing youth camps and preaching all over the Visayas and Mindanao. Many young people came to the Lord and were baptized with the Holy Spirit. Several went to Bible school.

One of the encouraging things that resulted from this was seeing the response of the Filipinos. The Lord helped them build relationships with pastors and leaders in their area of ministry such that the local churches started supporting the Bible school. By the time they left IBI in 1975, student population went from 30 to a high of 116; US funding went from 75% to 25%. The rest of the school funds were locally raised. Moreover, the school had Missions Conventions every year. As students learned to trust God and give to missions, they experienced supernatural provision for their own needs.

APTS and Beyond – 1977 to Present

It was Everett's great privilege to serve as President of Far East Advanced School of Theology (FEAST, now Asia Pacific Theological Seminary, APTS) from 1977-1984.[4] Back then, FEAST was a two-year BTh program designed to help graduates of three-year Bible schools throughout Asia Pacific complete a four-year degree. An extension program was also started to take the 4th year to a number of countries. Everett served both as President and Director of the Extension Program. The program became quite extensive under his direction. Meanwhile Evelyn served as Academic Dean and Dean of Students.[5]

As Bible colleges began to be able to provide their own BA programs, FEAST started to offer Master's programs in Theology and Christian Education. A two-year MTS program was designed. Thus, the school became a graduate level institution. It was also under Everett's leadership that the resident student population reached forty and facilities for student and faculty housing plus faculty offices became inadequate. It became clear that FEAST needed a bigger

---

[4] William Menzies and John F. Carter, *Zeal with Knowledge: The First Forty Years of FEAST/APTS* (Baguio City, Philippines: APTS Press, 2004), 19-20.

[5] McKinney Newsletter, December 1981, Asia Pacific Research Center, Asia Pacific Theological Seminary, Baguio City, Philippines.

campus. Thus Everett began surveying for possible campuses before going on furlough.[6]

The McKinneys realized they needed more training, so during their deputation time, they completed Master's degrees at the Assemblies of God Theological Seminary in Springfield, Missouri. They also accomplished all the resident requirements for the DMin. However, circumstances did not allow them to complete the doctoral projects.

In February 1985, Everett felt it was time to step aside to facilitate the selection of an Asian President.[7] However, they continued to teach at APTS as adjunct faculty after resigning as President. Moreover, for several years, Everett served as Director of Development and helped to coordinate the extension program.[8] This means that for the past forty-two years and counting, the McKinneys have been ministering at APTS.

About the time of Everett's resignation, the Lord began to speak to the couple about being willing to move out of their comfort zone into a ministry that would take them to many countries, Bible colleges, and seminaries. Presently, they teach block courses at APTS in Baguio City, Philippines; Continental Theological Seminary in Brussels, Belgium; Southern Asia Bible College in Bangalore, India; and Evangel Theological Seminary in Kiev, Ukraine.[9]

Consequently, for the last nearly thirty years, the McKinneys have been traveling twelve months of the year and living a "homeless" lifestyle, with one suitcase and one computer bag each. Currently they headquarter in Singapore and have a few things stored there. They are fifteen years past normal retirement age, and their ministry schedule is full two years ahead. They feel incredibly blessed!

Others who witness the McKinneys' current lifestyle living out of a suitcase are just as blessed. Dickie Hertweck, a missionary colleague, comments, "They are very adaptable and flexible. They have lived in our house at APTS for months when we've been away. Evelyn is so cute

---

[6]Menzies and Carter, 21.
[7]McKinney Resignation Letter, Feb. 4, 1985, Asia Pacific Research Center, Asia Pacific Theological Seminary, Baguio City, Philippines.
[8]Menzies and Carter, 23.
[9]See McKinneys resumé in the appendices.

when she comments how nice it is to 'play house' and unpack their suitcases. . . . [Their attitude simply] shows the students/faculty that material things are secondary."[10]

For Judy Cagle Higgins, a former APTS President's wife, the McKinneys "have lived a life of sacrifice, travel, and a desire to minister wherever God opened the doors . . . Material goods have played a very small part of their lives. They lived for eternal values."[11]

Gary Goh, a former student at Assemblies of God Bible College (now ACTS) Singapore, believes "their chosen lifestyle to serve God, away from comforts of retirement, exemplify a lifelong devotion that many generations of believers can learn from."[12]

Physical Challenges

From 1976 to 1978, while serving as President of FEAST, Everett endured worsening dizzy spells. Neurologists determined that he had atrophy of the brain – his brain cells were dying rapidly, but the doctors didn't have a cure for him.

Everett's eyes and balance were affected. He could read only a bit at a time. He preached holding onto the pulpit. Evelyn read to him so he could teach his class. Often, Evelyn would go into his office and they would earnestly pray and ask God to touch him and help him make it through the day. Evelyn did all the driving for the family since their sons, Doug and Steve, were only seven and nine years old at that time. Those eighteen months were the longest and darkest trial of their lives; they feared their missionary career and ministry was finished.[13]

One night, in a missionary prayer meeting, Paul Klahr asked for prayer for Everett who would be going to the US for treatment. As the missionaries prayed, Everett was standing alone. Feeling hands on the back of his head, he turned to see who laid hands on him, but nobody was there. He then knew Jesus touched him. Yet, the next day, he was

---

[10]Dickie Hertweck, response to Questionnaire, received May 7, 2018.
[11]Judy Cagle Higgins, response to Questionnaire, received May 8, 2018.
[12]Gary Goh, response to Questionnaire, received May 11, 2018. He is President of Society for Asian Foresight Education, Singapore.
[13]Everett McKinney, "President's Report to the Board of Directors, 1978-79", Asia Pacific Research Center, Asia Pacific Theological Seminary, Baguio City, Philippines.

as dizzy as ever. Everett was afraid that going home would negate his faith, but he was advised to go. Finally, back in the US, after going through all the tests, the doctors told him, "Yes, you had a problem, but you don't now. Go slowly off this medication and get back to work." That was forty years ago!

Evelyn had her own physical challenge. Twenty-eight years ago, she had colon cancer. The miracle for her was that it was discovered before it had spread. With people undergirding them with prayer Evelyn had surgery in the US while Everett stayed in Malaysia to teach. God answered those prayers: five weeks after the surgery, Evelyn and Everett were on their way to Portugal and India!

The most recent bout with sickness happened to Everett in 2016 when he was diagnosed with lymphoma. His spleen, stomach, liver, and pancreas were full of cancerous tumors. The doctor said there was only a 30-35% chance that chemotherapy would work, but they should try. Again the Lord spoke to Everett, "Fight! Don't give up!" So they did.

Everett testified that during those very difficult eighteen weeks, God repeatedly spoke to him, saying, "Trust Me. I know what I'm doing," and "I am not finished with you yet. You are not ready to cross the finish line. When your time comes, you will know it, and it will be good."

During this process, the McKinneys had to cancel seven months of their ministry schedule in Russia, Mongolia, a sensitive country that cannot be named, Myanmar, and APTS. Everett's prayer during this time was: "Lord, you extended my life forty years ago. I ask you to do it again so that I can accomplish every purpose for which you called me." People around the world prayed with them, and the cancer is in remission today![14]

Early in 2018, the Lord once again spoke to Everett. He was having bouts of doubt when something about his body did not seem to be quite right. The Lord came with this reassuring promise that He will complete the healing process: "I have healed you; I am healing you; and I will heal you." God has promised, and that is all that they need.

---

[14]After 5 weeks of treatment, Everett and Evelyn went back to the ministry with 80% of Everett's $400,000 medical bill shouldered by Medicare – another of God's wonderful provisions!

The McKinneys have been able to reschedule all of the cancelled ministries and are going strong. Everett declared with deep conviction: "Looking back to my early years—the supernatural encounters, and two supernatural extensions of life—all these were the driving force that moves us on when we face crisis times. Sure, we are affected, but we come back stronger and more useful in the Kingdom."

Blessings in the Mission Field

When asked what they liked most in the ministry, the McKinneys mentioned two things: the fruit of the ministry and the relationships and friendships they have formed.

Fruit of the Ministry

It is clear in their ministry that the McKinney's highest priority is "reaching the lost and training the found," and they see education as the key. As FEAST President, Everett "gave particular attention to preparing students to function in Christian education and Bible school training programs, which was consistent with his stated conviction that training Asians for leadership was the key to evangelizing Asia."[15] He thus wrote, "The unprecedented, sovereign move of the Holy Spirit in Asia demands that Asian leaders be prepared to reap and preserve the fruit of evangelism, and that continues to be our goal at FEAST."[16] Evelyn adds, "And then going into churches – whether large or small – and seeing pastors who are pouring their lives into people the way we wanted to pour our lives into them – there is nothing more rewarding." It is no surprise that both colleagues and students declare that the McKinneys were "teachers after God's own heart."

Dickie Hertweck vouches for their love for the students. She witnessed how they would go into a classroom or meeting room before class time and "pray over each chair, desk, and student who will sit

---

[15] Dave Johnson, "FEAST/APTS in Retrospect Part 1: The Manila Years (1964-1986)," *AJPS*, 17:1 (2014), 9.
[16] Everett L. McKinney, "Leadership Training at FEAST", *Mountain Movers*, August 1982, 4.

there."¹⁷ Judy Cagle had the privilege of co-teaching with Evelyn in APTS. She said Evelyn shared everything with her, thus she learned a lot from one she considers a "master teacher."¹⁸

Greek is a difficult class to teach, but Casey Ng and Davina Soh, Evelyn's students at APTS, greatly enjoyed her Greek 2 class because she made the difficult subject fun with her personal examples and humor. Even the final exam was fun because the students enjoyed her popcorn, cake, cookies and punch.¹⁹ Roli dela Cruz, Evelyn's former FEAST student, now a Greek professor himself, says that it was Evelyn's warmth as a teacher, her ability to make difficult Greek classes fun through her sense of humor, and her natural kindness and sincerity that he wants to emulate in his own teaching ministry.²⁰ Cina Bozarth Silva took Creative Teaching under Evelyn. She declared, "[It] was the best and most practical class of my college years!"²¹

Everett and Evelyn see the fruit of their teaching and training going on long after they are gone. They are delighted that, for the last several years, they have regularly helped to train Asian and Eastern European nationals from many countries. For example, some of their Filipino students became missionaries in Laos and Cambodia. They believe Asian missionaries can often do a better job than Western missionaries in Asia because they can mingle more easily. Adapting is easier for them because Asian cultures are more similar. From two missionary training schools in Romania where the McKinneys teach every year, there are now seventy Romanian missionaries in tough places like Afghanistan, Northern India, Namibia and Niger in Africa, Egypt, and Macedonia.

---

    ¹⁷Dickie Hertweck, response to Questionnaire.
    ¹⁸Higgins, response to Questionnaire.
    ¹⁹Casey Ng and Davina Soh, response to Questionnaire, received May 7, 2018. This couple are now lecturers at ACTS College (formerly Assemblies of God Bible College), Singapore.
    ²⁰Roli G. dela Cruz, response to Questionnaire, received May 25, 2018. Dr. Dela Cruz is presently Associate Professor of New Testament at Vanguard University, CA, USA.
    ²¹Cina Silva, response to Questionnaire, received September 26, 2018. She and her husband, Ty, are Co-Pastors at Agape International Christian Assembly, Taipei, and serve as AGWM Area Directors for the Northern Pacific Rim.

In one of his reflections, Everett had this to say:

> Leadership development is not a quick-fix for challenging church problems. It is a very rewarding long-range process. How exciting it is to look at the products—the fruit—of 40 years of "developing Spirit-led leaders." I see them all over Asia and the Pacific, and even beyond, serving capably as Bible school presidents, deans, and faculty members, general superintendents and executive officers, pastors, and church planters. I see Asian missionaries serving in different countries of the world with great acceptance and distinction.[22]

Relationships and Friendships

For the McKinneys, one of the key factors that contribute to the success of missionaries in the field has to do with relationships: relationships with the national church, missionary-missionary relationships, all kinds of relationships. They certainly live up to what they believe as proven by their characteristics observed by those who know the couple well. Here are but a few:

> "Strengths: academicians, scholastic, adaptable, sacrificial, friendly"[23]
> "Strengths: humility, dedication, self-sacrifice"[24]
> "Self-giving. Patient. Giving room for growth and development."[25]

---

[22] Everett L. McKinney, "Reflections of a Former President," in *Reflections on Developing Asian Pentecostal Leaders: Essays in Honor of Harold Kohl*, A. Kay Fountain, ed. (Baguio City, Philippines: APTS Press, 2004), 29.

[23] Marcus Tan, response to Questionnaire, received June 21, 2018. He is Senior Pastor of Penang First Assembly of God, Penang, Malaysia.

[24] Galen Hertweck, response to Questionnaire, received May 7, 2018. He is an APTS faculty member.

[25] Anthony Phua, response to Questionnaire, received May 7, 2018. He is an APTS Adjunct faculty member.

"They are very positive and gentle, friendly and personal. They do not carry airs with them as missionaries or superiors."[26]

"Soft hearted persons. Generous to the needy. They are very approachable."[27]

The McKinneys established relationships both inside and outside the classroom. Gary Goh shares the impact the McKinneys had on his life:

> I first met them in my first module in ACTS College. Back then, I had just returned to the Lord after a ten-year departure from faith, and felt led to enroll in Bible School. In that first lesson, seated among many pastors and mature believers, I felt inadequate and uncertain. But the McKinneys' compassion and encouragement eased me into the academic life in Bible college. I recalled Rev. Everett McKinney said at that first lesson, "Some things are caught rather than taught." I thank God that He sent His servants to help me catch the passion of serving Christ.[28]

Casey and Davina were recipients of the couple's hospitality in APTS:

> We remember the hospitality of the McKinneys when we were in their small group. We remember the taco press that Bro. McKinney would use to make fresh tacos for dinner. We also remember the carrot cake that Sis. McKinney bakes. And it was always fun to hear Sis. McKinney tell stories and sing songs. Davina's dissertation is "The Motif of Hospitality in Theological Education." The various ways the McKinneys expressed hospitality certainly played a part when she was conceptualizing her dissertation topic—what theological

---

[26] Yoot Wah Yeang, response to Questionnaire, received May 21, 2018. He is a retired pastor and Bible College lecturer.

[27] Maria Mercedes "Mercy" Panelo, response to Questionnaire, received August 17, 2018. She is an administrative assistant at APTS.

[28] Goh, response to Questionnaire.

educators can do to practice hospitality within and without the theological classrooms.[29]

The couple also established relationships with the school workers. Mercy Panelo, an APTS staff, is very grateful that the couple treats her as their daughter and even visited her family in their humble abode. They see to it that her family would fellowship with them each time they come to APTS.

Most of all, the McKinneys were willing to make sacrifices way beyond expectations for their relationships, and this was demonstrated through the Ibañez siblings. Zenaida and her siblings were orphans so her eldest sister, a student at IBI, brought all three sisters and one brother to Cebu City. Zenaida was seventeen years old when the McKinneys came in 1969. The couple took her in as their working student. In this way, she experienced firsthand the couple's loving kindness, patience, and generosity.[30]

When the McKinneys heard of the miserable life of Zenaida's siblings, Nena, Nelly, and Boy, they took all three children home to live with them. Soon the siblings were calling them "*Tatay*" and *Nanay*" McKinney. Of the three, Nelly was an especially difficult child —stubborn and hardheaded, but the McKinneys were very loving, kind, patient, and understanding, praying for her salvation during the nightly family devotions. Nelly testified: "After three years of interceding for me (I was 12 years old), I received the Lord and was baptized in the Holy Spirit during one of the evening services of the one week Missions Convention in IBI. The Lord answered their prayers; I was a changed person."[31]

The McKinneys' loving kindness and generosity went further still. To Zenaida's amazement and deep gratitude, a week before her wedding, Everett and Evelyn told her that they have decided to adopt her and her two younger sisters, Nena and Nelly! *Tatay* Everett gave her away on her wedding day. And when she gave birth to her first

---

[29]Ng and Soh, response to Questionnaire.
[30]Zenaida Ibañez Olayvar, response to Questionnaire, received Aug. 25, 2018. She became Senior Pastor of Toledo Assembly of God Church after the death of her husband.
[31]Nelly Ibañez, response to Questionnaire, received Aug. 31, 2018. She is presently the District Secretary of the Eastern Visayas District Council of the PGCAG.

born, *Nanay* Evelyn took her and her baby home for one week so she could help care for them. Moreover, throughout Zenaida's pioneering and church planting ministry with her husband, Rosendo, the McKinneys were their constant supporters. Up to the present, the couple would visit her family whenever they come to Cebu. Zenaida gratefully said, "We have truly felt the love of God through them."[32] Both Zenaida and Nelly are thankful that Everett and Evelyn are their "God-given parents."[33]

With these multiple ways by which they touched lives, it is no wonder that some of their colleagues consider them as "heroes."[34] And if ever anyone would fault them, it would be in what one termed as being "too kind"[35] and being "very self-giving" that they sometimes have less time for themselves and their family.[36] One close observer lamented that people have taken advantage of their kindness and generosity.[37] However, Roli believes that "it is most likely that it is their natural kindness to people that prevails in the manner in which they relate and minister to students."[38]

Yet, despite their multiple accomplishments as veteran missionaries, the McKinneys maintain, "We are far from the ideal. We have made our share of mistakes. But people know that we love them, and that our intentions are good. So we are able to work out misunderstandings. We cherish precious friendships we have today—some going back fifty years!"

Messages from the McKinneys

Everett and Evelyn were asked, "Given a chance to address the local ministers, what important message would you tell them?" They were likewise asked the same question addressed to their own family. Below are their messages:

---

[32]Olayvar, response to Questionnaire.
[33]Olayvar and Ibañez, in their responses to their questionnaires.
[34]Galen Hertweck, Judy Cagle Higgins, Maria Mercedes "Mercy" Panelo, Zenaida Olavar, and Nelly Ibañez all said this in their responses to Questionnaire.
[35]Dela Cruz, response to Questionnaire.
[36]Phua and Ibañez, in their questionnaires.
[37]Olayvar, response to Questionnaire.
[38]Dela Cruz, response to Questionnaire.

To Ministers/Pastors

Everett: My desire is to live every day as if it is my last day on earth, preach every sermon and teach every class as if it is my last—because that time will come. I don't know when that is. But I want to be ready to stand before the Lord with clean hands and a pure heart. I try to live with the finish line in focus.

Evelyn: The most important thing I've learned is that, in myself, I can do nothing; I must depend on the power of the Holy Spirit. I must be so in tune with the Father that I can "see" what He is doing. I need the empowerment of the Spirit to empower me, to give me words to say, to give me right attitude, and to work in the hearts of those who hear His words. Without the power of the Spirit, it's worthless.

To Their Family

Evelyn: I want my children and grandchildren to meet me in heaven one day. I'll be waiting at the Eastern Gate. I want them to understand that the Christian life is the life of minimum regrets. It's the life that is most rewarding. Jesus is real! Love Him! Serve Him! Be faithful!

Everett: I have had a full and complete life. It hasn't always been easy, but it has been good, and Jesus has been with us every step of the way. Our missionary call has taken us away from you, our family, sometimes for long periods. We know that you don't have the same missions call that we did, but we have tried to maintain a good relationship with you. I believe there will be many people who will say to you, "I wouldn't be here if your parents had not worked to win me, train me, and encourage me."

I'm ready to go to heaven, but I would feel very bad if I won and trained thousands, and anyone in my own family would not be there. Please make sure that your relationship with God is intact. I want our family to be together for eternity.

Conclusion

Everett and Evelyn penned the following as their Philosophy of Ministry:

Everett and Evelyn McKinney are driven by the Biblical mandate to preach the Gospel and make disciples in every nation. Recognizing that this cannot be done by missionaries alone, they are called and committed to training national ministers, leaders, Bible school teachers, Christian educators, and missionaries. Following the ministry model of Jesus and Paul, they seek to train "faithful men and women" who will then teach others.[39]

For about half a century, more than half of their earthly lives, the McKinneys have labored in the mission field, crisscrossing more than 100 countries in several continents. Through the years, they have remained faithful to this mandate. As APTS celebrates their life and ministry, three of their colleagues pay them tribute below:

Roli dela Cruz

In behalf of my family, I would like to express our encouragement and appreciation to them for all that they have done for the work of the Lord in the Asia-Pacific region. Their dedication and commitment to the work of the Lord, although they are technically retired, inspires and encourages me to keep on going and not to get weary in the service of the Lord Jesus Christ as nothing done for the work of God will ever be wasted. And I am a product of their hard work for the kingdom of God![40]

---

[39]Taken from "Introduction to the Ministry of Everett and Evelyn McKinney", sent to this writer by Everett McKinney, April 24, 2018.
[40]Dela Cruz, response to Questionnaire.

Cina Silva

The McKinneys had a profound impact on my life and ministry. . . . I saw them to be true servant leaders who sincerely respected the co-workers they were responsible to lead at IBC (then IBI). Beyond the academic and administrative leadership they provided, the McKinneys wholistically cared for the students, staff and faculty.[41]

Judy Cagle Higgins

The McKinneys have been pioneers in the development of Christian education resources and preaching materials. Their passing their passion and pursuit of excellence in ministry on to students around the world is their legacy. We have been privileged as a Pentecostal movement to have their dedication and expertise. They have truly influenced a whole generation of Pentecostal leaders worldwide.[42]

Indeed, when the day comes that we will all be standing around God's throne, many of us will be joining the multitude of saints who will be thanking Everett and Evelyn McKinney for the generations of believers who were touched by their ministry.

---

[41] Silva, response to Questionnaire.
[42] Higgins, response to Questionnaire.

TELL IT TO YOUR CHILDREN'S CHILDREN

Kay Fountain

I am honoured to write this article to celebrate the McKinney's ministry in Asia. I believe that they truly epitomise the kind of teachers that God requires to teach the younger generation. I have been blessed to be in their classes and to share their lives. They truly fulfil the biblical requirements for theological education.

There are several passages in the Old Testament which refer to passing on to the next generation the things that have been learned and experienced by the current generation. These must surely be amongst the earliest records of theological education in Asia. This paper will examine nine such passages in detail and refer briefly to others. However, the exhortations in these passages are not only confined to the Old Testament, so it will also examine some New Testament texts and consider the current situation in the churches in Asia. The first three Old Testament passages are in Exodus, followed by four passages in Deuteronomy and the others come from Psalms and Joel.

In Exodus 10:1-2 "The Lord said to Moses, 'Go to Pharaoh, for I have hardened his heart and the hearts of his officials so that I may perform these miraculous signs of mine among them that you may tell your children and grandchildren how I dealt harshly with the Egyptians and how I performed my signs among them, and that you may know that I am the Lord.'"[1] The generation who saw the plagues that God inflicted upon the Egyptians were to tell the succeeding generations so that they would remember how God had judged Egypt and delivered Israel. Cole says "Faith is kindled by recounting the great 'triumphs of

---

[1] All Scripture references here are taken from the New International Version (NIV) of the Bible.

God' (Jdg. 5:10,11), in this case His *signs*. . . ."[2] Noth, however, simply mentions that Pharaoh's " . . . 'stubbornness' is the occasion of the ever-renewed miraculous signs, which are afterwards to be handed down in Israel from generation to generation."[3] It is clear that the focus of most commentators is actually on the content of the plagues. However, for the purposes of this paper, I am placing the emphasis on the passing on of faith to the following generations. By recounting God's punishment of Egypt to the generations after them, the Israelites were to inspire their children to follow the Lord and to enjoy His protection and blessing.

Exodus 13:8 speaks of the celebration of the Passover: "On that day tell your son 'I do this because of what the Lord did for me when I came out of Egypt.'" The celebration of the Passover was not simply a feast, but an opportunity for educating the younger generation. In fact, this was really the purpose for all of the feasts. Exodus 13:14 refers to the redemption of the firstborn saying "In days to come, when your son asks you, 'What does this mean?' say to him, 'with a mighty hand the LORD brought us out of Egypt, out of the land of slavery.'" These two texts show that the ritual practices that God required of the Israelites were to be used as teaching moments in the lives of the generations to follow. They were not merely memorials, or celebrations, but opportunities to build faith and understanding in the younger generation. God required that parents explain the rituals, and the reason for them to their children.

In Deuteronomy 4:9 we read, "Only be careful, and watch yourselves closely so that you do not forget the things your eyes have seen or let them slip from your heart as long as you live. Teach them to your children and to their children after them." Here the Israelites are commanded to remember what they have *seen*—the destruction of the Egyptians, their escape through the Red Sea, the manna, and the water from the rock, the provision of the quail, and also the punishments that God had given to those who disobeyed. They were to tell their children

---

[2]R. Alan Cole, *Exodus, an Introduction & Commentary,* Tyndale Old Testament Commentaries, D. J. Wiseman, General Editor. (Intervarsity Press, Leicester, England, 1973), 99.

[3]Martin Noth, *Exodus: A Commentary,* The Old Testament Library, Translated by J.S. Bowden. (The Westminster Press, Philadelphia, 1962), 82.

and grandchildren about these things. In order to remember those things they had seen, they would have to repeat them again and again. The mighty acts of God were to be retold, generation after generation. "Moreover the faithful transmission of the story to the children was obligatory for Israel (*cf* Ex. 13:8, 14)."[4]

Then in Deuteronomy 6:6-7 we read:

> These commandments that I give you today are to be upon your hearts. Impress them on your children. Talk about them when you sit at home and when you walk along the road, when you lie down and when you get up. Tie them as symbols on your hands and bind them on your foreheads. Write them on the doorframes of your houses and on your gates.

Here the Israelites are instructed to impress upon their children the *commandments* that God had given them. Thompson indicates that,

> The book of Deuteronomy attaches a special importance to this task of teaching the family (4:9b; 6:20-25; 11:19). But the demands of Yahweh's covenant are to be the subject of conversation at all times in the home, by the way, by night and by day. Israel is to *teach them diligently, talk of them* constantly, *bind them as a sign* on various parts of the body, and *write them*. God's love and His covenant demands were to be the central and absorbing interest of a man's whole life.[5]

God's commands were to be so much a part of their daily life that they would be impressed upon the children. This implies not only direct instruction, but also instruction by example. Referring to Deuteronomy 6:6-9, Maxwell says *"A person must experience the love this commandment requires before he or she can teach it to others."*[6] He continues:

---

[4] J.A. Thompson, *Deuteronomy, an Introduction & Commentary,* Tyndale Old Testament Commentaries, D. J. Wiseman, General Editor (Intervarsity Press, Leicester, England, 1974), 104.
[5] Ibid. 123.
[6] John C. Maxwell, *Deuteronomy,* The Communicator's Commentary, General Editor Lloyd J. Ogilvie (Word Books, Waco, Texas, 1987), 127.

This commandment is not automatically transferred from one generation to another. Deuteronomy attaches the importance and responsibility of teaching to the family (4:9; 6:7; 11:19). This educating must be done in a diligent manner. The home is to be the center for conserving and propagating truth. Home is where life makes up its mind. Moses understood that the greatness of the nation Israel depended upon the teaching of the commandments in the home.[7]

Again in Deuteronomy 11:18-21 Moses commands:

Fix these words of mine in your hearts and minds; tie them as symbols on your hands and bind them on your foreheads. Teach them to your children, talking about them when you sit at home and when you walk along the road, when you lie down and when you get up. Write them on the doorframes of your houses and on your gates, so that your days and the days of your children may be many in the land that the Lord swore to give your fathers, as many as the days that the heavens are above the earth.

This time they are instructed to teach the commandments which Moses had given them, however, these commands came from the Lord through Moses, so the content of the teaching is the same as in the previous passage. Thompson says "Since obedience to Yahweh was fundamental for Israel's well-being, the commandments of Moses needed to be laid up in the heart of the present generation and carefully transmitted to future generations."[8] Maxwell emphasises the importance of this continual reminder to the next generation as follows:

---

[7]Ibid. 128.
[8]Thompson, 155.

Experts in the field of communications say that our learning is 89 percent visual, 10 percent auditory, and 1 percent through the other senses. Moses wanted to make sure that family members continually had the law *"in your heart and in your soul."* The continual reading, teaching and discussion of God's word would bring blessing.[9]

Finally in Deuteronomy 32:46 we read "He said to them, 'Take to heart all the words I have solemnly declared to you this day, so that you may command your children to obey carefully all the words of this law.'" They are reminded again that they must remember God's commandments and teach their children to obey them. It is not enough to simply teach them the commands, they must teach them obedience to the commands. As Maxwell says "A healthy fear of judgment will also help their descendants to obey God's word."[10] Teaching the next generation obedience, however, is not something that can be done only by talking. Children will learn to obey God's commands when they see their parents walking in obedience. It is a question of modelling the desired behaviour. If the commands are taught but not obeyed by the parents, the children may learn the commands, but they will also not obey.

But Psalm 78:3-7 talks about what happens when the parents both teach and obey:

What we have heard and known, what our fathers had told us. We will not hide them from their children; we will tell the next generation the praiseworthy deeds of the Lord, his power and the wonders he had done. He decreed statutes for Jacob and established the law in Israel which he commanded our forefathers to teach their children, so the next generation would know them, even the children yet to be born, and they in turn would tell their children. Then they would put their trust in God and would not forget his deeds but would keep his commands.

---

[9]Maxwell, 176.
[10]Ibid. 337.

This shows the continued handing down from one generation to the next, both the things that the previous generation had experienced in their relationship to God, and the commands that they had received. It also calls for the teaching of younger generation so that they will not become stubborn like their fathers (v.8). Weiser contends that,

> What it wants to portray and impress on the mind is . . . the irrational quality of the things that have come to pass, in order that present and coming generations will bear in mind and never forget God's nature and will . . . together with the nature of human sin; simultaneously they are admonished to be faithful and obedient (v.7) and warned against unfaithfulness and fickleness (v.8), so that this knowledge will be preserved as a living force (vv. 4f.), as the holy tradition of God's covenant (vv. 10, 37).[11]

The last passage is in Joel 1:3 which says "Tell it to your children, and let your children tell it to their children, and their children to the next generation." In this final passage the elders in the land are commanded to make sure that the generations following them know what happened to them, and why it happened. It is a prophetic word about the judgment which will come upon the nation of Judah because of their sinfulness and refusal to repent. Normally, the Israelites were encouraged to tell the future generations about God's great acts of deliverance and protection, but in this passage, they are to pass on to the younger generation the memory of a disaster. It is to be a warning for the following generations to make sure that they do not make the mistakes of their elders. Hubbard explains "The incomparable event, as yet unnamed, is to be 'recounted' . . . , suggesting a detailed enumeration to generations following."[12] This is no simple, one-time lesson. It is to be repeated in detail so that the generations that follow will learn the lesson well. Not only must the Israelites teach their

---

[11] Artur Weiser, *The Psalms*, The Old Testament Library, trans. Herbert Hartwell (The Westminster Press, Philadelphia, 1962), 538.

[12] David Alan Hubbard, *Joel & Amos: An Introduction & Commentary*, Tyndale Old Testament Commentaries, D.J. Wiseman, General Editor (Inter-varsity Press, Leicester, England, 1989), 42.

children about God's blessings that they have received, but they must also make it very clear to their children that God disciplines and that disasters that befall them may be because they have deserted God and have not fulfilled the requirements of covenant faithfulness.

All of these passages clearly place the responsibility for theological education squarely within the context of the home. As Kidner says ". . . Scripture has no room for parental neutrality."[13]

The New Testament also impresses this responsibility upon parents. Ephesians 6:4 says "Fathers do not exasperate your children; instead, bring them up in the training and instruction of the Lord." Alister McGrath states,

> Here *training* is a comprehensive word; it means the training or education of a child, including the whole process of instruction and discipline. *Instruction*, "to put in mind," is included under the more general term and can be correctly translated "admonition." It is the act of reminding one of his faults or duties. Children are not to be allowed to grow up without care or control. They are to be instructed, disciplined and admonished, so that they are brought to knowledge, self-control, and obedience. This whole process of education is to be religious, and not only religious but Christian.[14]

Believing parents are responsible for the theological education of their children. This is not a task that can be left to the church or Sunday School. While there is clearly a place for the Church, the Bible School, and the Seminary to continue that education, the basis of their theological understanding must be taught in the home by believing parents. Bruce says:

> The "training and instruction of the Lord" would involve following Christ's example, with due regard to his 'meekness and gentleness' (2 Cor.10:1), as well as putting into practice his precepts. And the children will the more readily learn these

---

[13]Derek Kidner, *Psalms 73-150*, Tyndale Old Testament Commentaries, D.J. Wiseman, General Editor (Inter-varsity Press, Leicester, England, 1975), 281.

[14]Alister McGrath, *Ephesians*, The Crossway Classic Commentaries, Alister McGrath and J.I. Packer, Series Editors (Crossway Books, Wheaton, Illinois, 1994), 203-4.

lessons if the parents themselves show the way—by following Christ's example and practicing his precepts.[15]

It is clear then, that God's commands to the Israelites clearly state the necessity of theological education, and that the context for that education is in the home. Paul's exhortation to the Ephesians expresses the same sentiments. Believing parents have the responsibility before God, to give their children a thorough theological education.

In examining these passages further, we can find some guidelines for both the content of the theological education that parents were responsible for, and the method by which they were to teach. The content of the education in Deuteronomy 4:9 is the things that the Israelites have seen, the mighty, miraculous acts of God in the Exodus event. In Deut. 6:6 the content is "These commandments that I give you today," which is reiterated in the other passages in Deuteronomy. In the Psalm the content is both what they have experienced and also what they have been told by previous generations and in Joel, the content of the instruction is the judgment which God was bringing upon them, and the reason for that judgment.

The first responsibility is for the parents is to share with their children what God has done in their own lives. Their own experience of God's miraculous power, both for deliverance and discipline, should be recounted to the next generation. Second, they are to take God's commandments to heart. Third, they are to teach not only the commandments, but obedience to them. While teaching the commands can be done by passing on the information, teaching obedience to the commands must be done by modelling. The passage in Ephesians also indicates the necessity of this instruction, and makes it clear that it must be ongoing and thorough.

Hence we see that the Old Testament model for theological education is for parents to teach their children, and their grandchildren three things: their own experience of God's mighty acts, both for

---

[15]F.F. Bruce, *The Epistles to the Colossians to Philemon and to the Ephesians*, The New International Commentary on the New Testament (William B. Eerdmans Publishing Company, Grand Rapids, Michigan, 1984), 398-9.

deliverance and for judgment, God's commandments, and obedience to God's commandments.

The method for this education is also given, particularly in Deuteronomy 6 and 11. God's instruction is for parents to include His commandments in their entire life. They should not only talk about them, they should give them a place of honour. They should be foremost in their minds, whatever activity they are involved in. They should not only share by active instruction with their children, but they should live out their lives in such a way that the children will see that God's commands are the basis for all of their life and all of their behaviour. Not only is this a direct instruction to Israelite parents, but in other places in the Old Testament (e.g. Deut. 6:20-25) it is presumed that children will ask their parents questions and that the parents will be ready with a response. In Exodus 12:24-27 Moses commanded:

> Obey these instructions as a lasting ordinance for you and your descendants. When you enter the land that the Lord will give you as he promised, observe this ceremony. And when your children ask you "What does this ceremony mean to you?" Then tell them, "It is the Passover sacrifice to the Lord, who passed over the houses of the Israelites in Egypt and spared our homes when he struck down the Egyptians." Then the people bowed down and worshiped.

The annual celebration of the Passover was supposed to prompt the children to ask their parents its meaning. In Joshua 4:4-7 we are told:

> So Joshua called together the twelve men who had been appointed from the Israelites, one from each tribe, and said to them, "Go over before the ark of the Lord your God into the middle of the Jordan. Each of you is to take up a stone on his shoulder according to the number of the tribes of the Israelites, to serve as a sign among you. In the future, when your children ask you, "What do these stones mean?" tell them that the flow of the Jordan was cut off before the ark of the covenant of the Lord. When it crossed the Jordan, the waters of the Jordan

were cut off. These stones are to be a memorial to the people of Israel forever."

The memorial stones heaped up beside the Jordan river were supposed to prompt the children to ask their parents why they were there, and what was significant about this pile of stones. So we see that the method of instruction was not only teaching verbally about what God had done and commanded, but also living out the commandments in everyday life as an example, and in continually celebrating and making memorial monuments which would prompt questions from those who did not themselves experience the events.

Summarising we have the who, the what and the how of theological education. Parents are responsible for teaching their children. They should teach them what they have experienced of God's mighty acts, the judgments they have seen of those who are disobedient, both Israelite and non-Israelite, the commandments of God, and obedience to those commands. The method they are to use is not only verbal instruction, but modelling a lifestyle of obedience, and making celebrations and monuments what will give the children opportunity to ask questions.

One of the things that has been a great concern to me in my twenty-five years in the Philippines, but also in contact with other emerging nations, like Mongolia, Myanmar, and Cambodia, is the lack of parental responsibility in this area. Many parents are absent, overseas or working to provide a better financial future for their children. Art and Minda Elbinias estimate the number of documented OFWs from the Philippines at approximately 1 million, but if undocumented OFWs are included the total could be as high as 7 million."[16] The problem with this is that God has made parents responsible for the theological education of their children. If the parents are absent, where will the children obtain the education that leads them into meaningful relationship with God through Christ? This is a responsibility which cannot be abdicated to the church. God holds parents responsible as the primary theological educators of their

---

[16] "Mom's Make a Difference." Article in Mom's magazine, Issue 4, 2005.

children. Jesus asked this question of those who were his followers: "What good will it be for a man if he gains the whole world yet forfeits his soul?" This question might be rephrased to those who are seeking so earnestly to provide a better financial future for their children "What good will it be for the children who have everything they need financially, but do not learn to obey the Lord?" Theological education begins in the home. God has made it clear that he holds parents responsible for the theological education of their children. If parents work hard to provide financially but are absent and unable to pass on to their children their own experience of God's miraculous provision, they are failing in their responsibility. The Elbinias also state "Perhaps the most helpless victims of the separation are the children of OFWs. Minda reports that some kids, without parental presence, turn to drugs or early marriage. Without the presence of their parents, children are vulnerable to abuse by relatives or other household members they stay with."[17]

This is not simply an Old Testament requirement. In reference to Deuteronomy 4:9 Thompson states,

> The appeal to Israel "to remember and not to forget" God's saving acts is made again and again in Deuteronomy, for they were the foundation of Israel's claim to be God's people and the basis on which God challenged Israel to enter into His covenant. The same principle applies in the New Testament, where the acts of God in Christ are absolutely fundamental for the church and lie at the basis of God's appeal to men to enter into a new relationship with Himself. They too are to be taught to the children of believers.[18]

This is not merely only inferred from the Old Testament passages but is the clear teaching of the New Testament as well (Eph. 6:4). The ability to teach one's children well is also seen as a requirement for leadership in the church (1 Tim 3:4; 3:12; 5:10) for both men and women. It is therefore, essential that believing parents be present with

---

[17]Ibid.
[18]Thompson, 104.

their children, and instruct them by word and by example, to follow the Lord's commands.

Since, however, so many homes lack a parental example the church becomes responsible. This is also the case for new believers, who may have lacked a godly upbringing. In the church, the Bible school and the seminary it is clear that the first requirement is for the teachers to have meaningful relationship with the Lord. If the teachers have not submitted to the Lord's discipline, and had His laws written on their hearts, how can they possibly pass on to their students a biblically sound theological education? It is also clear that the method of instruction involves lifestyle as well as passing on information. Thus, as well as classroom instruction, there must be the opportunity for students to participate in the lives of their teachers. Teachers must open their lives to their students, so that they will learn from example as well as from verbal instruction. The who, what and how mentioned previously in relation to the instruction in the home, must continue in the Church, Sunday School, Bible school and seminary. Those who instruct others in theological education, must be 'spiritual' parents. They must take the place of the absent or unbelieving parent, and share their own experience of God's goodness, grace, discipline and provision. It is not enough to simply teach the precepts of God. the teacher must be a living example of one who follows God's word in their lifestyle.

Bibliography

Bruce, F.F. *The Epistles to the Colossians to Philemon and to the Ephesians*, The New International Commentary on the New Testament. William B. Eerdmans Publishing Company, Grand Rapids, Michigan, 1984.

Cole, R. Alan. *Exodus, an Introduction & Commentary*. Tyndale Old Testament Commentaries, D. J. Wiseman, General Editor. Intervarsity Press, Leicester, England, 1973.

Hubbard, David Alan. *Joel & Amos: An Introduction & Commentary*, Tyndale Old Testament Commentaries, D.J. Wiseman, General Editor. Inter-varsity Press, Leicester, England, 1989.

Kidner, Derek. *Psalms 73-150*, Tyndale Old Testament Commentaries, D.J. Wiseman, General Editor. Inter-varsity Press, Leicester, England, 1975.

Maxwell, John C. *Deuteronomy*. The Communicator's Commentary, General Editor Lloyd J. Ogilvie. Word Books, Waco, Texas, 1987.

McGrath, Alister. *Ephesians*, The Crossway Classic Commentaries, Alister McGrath and J.I. Packer, Series Editors. Crossway Books, Wheaton, Illinois, 1994.

"Moms make a difference." Article in Mom's magazine, Issue 4, 2005.

Noth, Martin. *Exodus: A Commentary*. The Old Testament Library. Translated by J.S. Bowden. The Westminster Press, Philadelphia, 1962.

Thompson, J.A. *Deuteronomy, an Introduction & Commentary*. Tyndale Old Testament Commentaries, D. J. Wiseman, General Editor. Intervarsity Press, Leicester, England, 1974.

Weiser, Artur. *The Psalms*, The Old Testament Library, Translated by Herbert Hartwell. The Westminster Press, Philadelphia, 1962.

LETTING GOD'S LOVE FORM OUR LIFE: Towards a Pentecostal Practice of Bible Reading

Monte Lee Rice

Introduction

Especially promising for 21st century Christian missional presence is the Pentecostal localizing giftedness that pluralizes Pentecostalism(s) worldwide.[1] However, detrimentally incongruent to this giftedness are some philosophical premises common in Pentecostal approaches to Scripture, primarily mediated via our Fundamentalist-Evangelical influences. I shall therefore address this incongruence by proposing a Pentecostal practice of Bible reading that comprises a form of *lectio divina* ('sacred reading') informed by Pentecostal distinctives.

To achieve this aim, I shall first survey the qualitative features of Pentecostal Bible reading (Part I). Next, I will address detriments to reading in ways incongruent to what I call this Pentecostal missionally localizing giftedness (Part II). Then I will delineate a Pentecostal practice of Bible reading informed by the historic Christian reading method known as *lectio divina* and, lastly, suggest how this Pentecostal

---

[1]Substantiating this suggestion is Dale T. Irvin's argument that, directly arising from the Pentecostal experience of Spirit baptism, is the inherent "logic of Pentecostal spirituality," resulting more often than not in the immediate localizing of Pentecostal global designs in the new situations of ministry outreach. Hence, he calls this logic of Pentecostal experience, the "localizing Pentecostal historical phenomenon." See Dale T. Irvin, "Pentecostal Historiography and Global Christianity: Rethinking the Question of Origins," *Pneuma*, 27, no. 1 (Spring 2005): 45.

form of *lectio divina* may help Pentecostals identify and utilise theological hermeneutics that best foster the Pentecostal missiological giftedness—and hence the pluralising of Pentecostalism(s) worldwide (Part III).

Part I: Qualitative Distinctives of Pentecostal Bible Reading

Let me begin by surveying four qualitative distinctives of Pentecostal Bible reading commonly observed in Pentecostal spirituality.

A first quality is that, over the past century, a hallmark of Pentecostalism that has funded its global vitality and role in the renewing of the Church Catholic has been an intuitive grasp of the 'plenary relevance' of the Bible. Hence, Pentecostals worldwide normally read the Bible as God's living Word, believing that, through the Holy Spirit's immediate illumination, we may find answers applicable to daily life and needs. At least at the grassroots level, this grasp of the Bible's immediate applicability has been historically nurtured through a concordinistic perception of Biblical truths and themes and hence a proof-texting pragmatic-oriented hermeneutic.[2] Pentecostals largely inherited these approaches from their historical links with the older Protestant Scholastic models of Bible doctrine and theology.

A second quality, which sometimes functions in tension with its pragmatic reading of Scripture, is a presumed polyvalence of meaning that Pentecostals grant to biblical texts, which they discern through spiritual illumination.[3]

A third quality has been what Frank Macchia defines as "a certain present-tenseness" that Pentecostals grant "to the events and words of the Bible, so that what happened then, happens now."[4]

---

[2] Andrew Davies, "What Does It Mean to Read the Bible as a Pentecostal?," *Journal of Pentecostal Theology* 18 (2009): 223; Allan H. Anderson, *An Introduction to Pentecostalism: Global Charismatic Christianity* (Cambridge, UK: Cambridge University Press, 2004), 225-227.

[3] Anderson, *An Introduction to Pentecostalism*, 226-228.

[4] Frank D. Macchia, "Theology, Pentecostal," in Stanley M. Burgess and Eduard M. van der Mass (eds.), *The New International Dictionary of Pentecostal and Charismatic Movements*, rev. ed. (Grand Rapids, MI: Zondervan Publishing House, 2002): 1122.

A fourth quality is the oral-aural epistemology and congregational ethos that is typical of Pentecostal congregational gatherings.[5] Relevant here is Kevin M. Bradt's defining of oral-aural (or "spoke-heard") events whereby, in their coming together, tellers and listeners create a space that generates imaginative power towards construction of new "story-worlds"; hence, a unique space wherein both teller and listener enter into a new future.[6] A robust Pentecostal oral-aural ethos therefore creates a heightened awareness of God's presence. This, in turn, creates a dialogical space wherein the participants anticipate miraculous and invasive ministerial manifestations of the Holy Spirit and heightened intuitiveness towards hearing and responding to the Word of the Lord.[7] Such events are thus intrinsic to the world-creating power of spoken prophetic words within the ethos of Pentecostal spirituality.[8]

To reiterate, I would affirm these four qualitative distinctives of Pentecostal Bible reading as intrinsic to a robust Pentecostal spirituality that is relevant to daily life needs through spiritual illumination, presumed polyvalence of meaning to biblical texts, existential identity within the biblical story-world, and an oral-aural epistemology that anticipates transforming encounters with the presence of God. Together, we can synthesise these distinctives as pointing towards an existentially dynamic assumption of Scriptural revelation and Bible reading.

Part II: Detriments to Pentecostal Bible Reading

I will now outline three detriments that often stand in tension to the qualitative distinctives I have just briefly surveyed. Given the historical links between Pentecostalism and Evangelicalism, the

---

[5]Walter J. Hollenweger, *Pentecostalism: Origins and Developments Worldwide* (Peabody, MA: Hendrickson Publishers, 1997), 2, 19-39, 112, 161, 177, 195-196, 269-278, 291-295, 322, 397-398.

[6]Kevin M. Bradt, *Story as a Way of Knowing* (Kansas City, KS: Sheed & Ward, 1997), 3-11, 14, 17.

[7]Daniel E. Albrecht, "Pentecostal Spirituality: Looking Through the Lens of Ritual," *Pneuma* 14, no. 2 (Fall 1992): 110-111, 114, 118-119.

[8]Jerry Camery-Hoggatt, "The Word of God from Living Voices: Orality and Literacy in the Pentecostal Tradition," *Pneuma* 27, no. 2 (Fall 2005): 225-226, 231, 238-239.

problems I raise largely mirror broader hermeneutical problematics of Protestant Evangelicalism.

Modernity's Foundationalist Quest for Scientific Certitude

The first detriment I would raise is modernity's foundationalist quest for scientific certitude. Much has been written on how the modern quest for scientific certitude has shaped the Protestant historical-grammatical approach to biblical interpretation and conversely, in both earlier liberal and conservative circles, the primary importance of authorial intent for determining the meaning of a biblical text. Hence, the locus of meaning was foundationally placed on the "message behind the text."[9]

The modern historical-grammatical stress on authorial intent as the most determinative meaning has always posed a recalcitrant tension with the dynamically open view of revelation that has been intrinsic to Pentecostal spirituality. Such a view worldwide has generally granted Pentecostals an attentive openness towards multiple meanings resident within Biblical texts.[10] Given the Pentecostal penchant for allegorising, there is certainly need for a hermeneutical control. Yet I would stress that the problem is not allegory *per se*, but rather allegorical readings coupled with the ahistorical biblical primitivism that distances Pentecostals from accessing ancient yet well-developed hermeneutical methods of guiding the meanings of allegorical or multi-sense readings of Scripture.

A Historical Biblical Primitivism

Positively, I should qualify this detriment by suggesting that fuelling the Pentecostal bent towards ahistorical biblical primitivism is the restorationist drive of Pentecostal spirituality. Historically, Pentecostals have often clarified this assumption via the term

---

[9]Stanley J. Grenz and John R. Franke, *Beyond Foundationalism: Shaping Theology in a Postmodern Context* (Louisville, KY: Westminster John Knox Press, 2001), 69-70.

[10]Dale M. Coulter, "What Meaneth This?: Pentecostals and Theological Inquiry," *Journal of Pentecostal Theology* 10, no. 1 (2001): 57; Anderson, *To the Ends of the Earth: Pentecostalism and the Transformation of World Christianity* (Oxford, UK: Oxford University Press, 2013), 121, 123.

'apostolic.'¹¹ Whereas historic church traditions, such as Roman Catholicism, may also define themselves as apostolic in the sense of sustaining continuity with the early church via faithfulness to the receiving and passing down of tradition, Pentecostals generally interpret apostolicity as experiencing restored intermediacy with the Church in the Book of Acts. Hence, this experience compels Pentecostals "to read Scripture in a restorationist manner."¹²

Therefore, their restorationist experience of apostolicity causes Pentecostals to read Scripture in an ahistorical manner. A critical downside to this ahistorical biblical primitivism, however, is a "modern chauvinism, which presumes whatever is premodern is likely to be relatively worthless" for present day believers.¹³ Ahistorical biblical primitivism thus robs Bible readers from enjoying the wisdom of Christian hermeneutical practices passed down through the ages within other Christian traditions, which can provide Pentecostals a seasoned repository of hermeneutical guidance in negotiating the polyvalent meanings of Scripture.¹⁴

Postmodern Pragmatic-Aimed Utilitarianism

The final detriment I will mention is what I call postmodern pragmatic-aimed utilitarianism. A helpful springboard for appreciating this dilemma is a contemporary contrast Lutheran theologian Oswald Bayer perceives to the classic Christian theological doctrine of God as the "God who communicates as our Maker."¹⁵ Bayer stresses how we should read Scripture as the 'holy space' where God our Maker also addresses us as our *Hermeneut*.¹⁶ Hence, in the holy space of Scripture

---

¹¹Steven Jack Land, *Pentecostal Spirituality: A Passion for the Kingdom* (JPTSup 1; Sheffield, UK: Sheffield Academic, 1993; Cleveland, TN: CPT, 2010), 3, 6; Macchia, *Baptized in the Spirit: A Global Pentecostal Theology* (Grand Rapids, MI: Zondervan, 2006), 229.

¹²Kenneth J. Archer, *A Pentecostal Hermeneutic: Spirit, Scripture and Community* (JPTSup 28; London, UK: Continuum, 2005; Cleveland, TN: CPT Press, 2009), 150-156.

¹³Thomas C. Oden, *Life in the Spirit*, Systematic Theology, vol. 3 (New York, NY: HarperSanFransicso; HarperCollins Publishers, 1994), 2.

¹⁴Grenz and Franke, *Beyond Foundationalism*, 109.

¹⁵Oswald Bayer, "Hermeneutical Theology," *Scottish Journal of Theology* 56 no. 2 (2003): 131.

¹⁶Ibid., 131, 138-146.

reading, He interprets us that He may form us into His likeness.[17] Yet often working against God's coming to us in His Word for this interpretive and thus formative purpose is the modern emphasis on self-actualisation. As a consequence, the aim of Scripture reading too often shifts from the proper posture of asking "How is God addressing us in the text?" to asking "How do I understand the given biblical text?"[18] Hence, "Appropriation has become more important than dedication" to God's formative aims through the reading of Scripture.[19]

Bayer's critique parallels Carl Raschke's contrast between a "propositional" and a "vocative" reading of Scripture. Whereas propositional reading tends to focus on questions of what a biblical text is about, vocative reading (using Martin Buber's communication model) is an I-Thou relational reading of Scripture.[20] Raschke thus reminds us to carefully avoid reading the Bible as if to presume it is a text about God, but rather as God actively addressing us[21] through which, in this very speech-act, He forms us in the way of salvation.

Part III: Premises for a Pentecostal Form of *Lectio Divina* Via a Trinitarian-Ontology of Scripture

The task that this analysis now points toward is to suggest a theological paradigm that nurtures the transformative qualities of Pentecostal Bible reading and the missiological giftedness of Pentecostalism, while effectively addressing the detriments I have just mentioned. The paradigm I will subsequently delineate emerges from a stronger ontological understanding of the Bible than what either Evangelicals or Pentecostals have normally articulated in their respective theologies or doctrines of Scripture—although I would argue that this ontology has probably implicitly existed within Pentecostal dynamic understandings of biblical revelation.

---

[17]Ibid., 131, 138-139, 142-143, 145-146.
[18]Ibid., 131.
[19]Ibid., 132.
[20]Carl Raschke, *The Next Reformation: Why Evangelicals Must Embrace Postmodernity* (Grand Rapids, MI: Baker Academic, 2004), 137-138.
[21]Ibid., 138.

Telford Work's Trinitarian-Ontology of Scripture

The specific theology of Scriptural ontology I am drawing on directly comes from Pentecostal theologian Telford Work's seminal bibliology titled, *Living and Active: Scripture in the Economy of Salvation*, which he describes as a Trinitarian ontology of Scripture.[22] This paradigm, which Work developed in manners that closely substantiate this essay's aims, suggests a distinctive Pentecostal practice of Bible reading informed by the historic Christian practice of *lectio divina*.

In recognising the need within Pentecostal tradition for a stronger ontology of the Bible, a major theological resource at hand is Simon Chan's consistent stress on the ontology of the Church, as prescriptive to the too common sociological or functional understanding that characterises much of Protestant Evangelical and Pentecostal ecclesiological thinking and practice. The fall-out Chan identifies within both of these traditions is a very utilitarian and consumerist orientation of the Church.[23] Ultimately what results is that the Church shifts from its purpose as the Spirit's creation of a *koinonia* that images God's trinitarian-shaped and redemptive mission in creation to (unfortunately) a community held together simply by a kindred human spirit. This kindred spirit is often formed by shared commitment to mutually agreed endeavours such towards aspired church growth and missionary outreach.[24] So in contrast to current sociological, functional, and hence utilitarian ideas of the Church, Chan stresses its ontological being-ness, which accentuates its reality as existing prior to creation (Eph 1:4) and thus its organic and relational existence as the body of Christ, who is its organic head.[25]

Chan's stress on ontology contrasts with the pragmatic modern tendency to define the Church strictly in utilitarian terms of

---

[22]Telford Work, *Living and Active: Scripture in the Economy of Salvation* (Grand Rapids, MI: William B. Eerdmans Publishing Co., 2002), 8, 10, 226.
[23]Simon Chan, *Pentecostal Theology and the Christian Spiritual Tradition* (JPTSup 21; Sheffield, UK: Sheffield Academic, 2000), 97-139; idem, "The Church and the Development of Doctrine," *Journal of Pentecostal Theology* 13, no. 1 (2004): 62-64.
[24]Chan, *Pentecostal Theology*, 98.
[25]Ibid., 97; "The Church and the Development of Doctrine," *Journal of Pentecostal Theology*, 63.

quantifiable achievement, where relevance then becomes of greater value than ontological fidelity as a witness to the Kingdom of God.[26] For this essay, an important implication of Chan's stress on the Church's ontology is an open and dynamic understanding of revelation from the Bible and existing within and throughout its life in history and nurtured through the interplay of "Spirit, Word, and Church."[27]

While Chan has not extended his ontology of the Church to a parallel understanding of the Bible, Work's Trinitarian ontology of Scripture provides the necessary transition. In doing so, Work has given us just the kind of theological paradigm that the issues presented in this paper necessitate for nurturing a Pentecostal reading of Scripture that is wholly congruent with a robust Pentecostal spirituality, which (I argue) should be more closely funded by theological themes characteristic of the ancient practice of *lectio divina*.[28]

Important to note are several crucial descriptions Work uses to characterise his bibliology, which he introduces as a "Trinitarian doctrine of Scripture that articulates the Bible's role in the divine economy of salvation," thus suggesting an understanding of Scripture via analogy to the Trinity. He argues from the premise that Scripture plays a determinative role in the "divine economy of salvation" and mirrors to us the Triunity of God and that "the Bible's character as the Word of God suggests a Trinitarian ontology of Scripture."[29] A major result Work delineates throughout the third part of his book is that the Bible's trinitarian ontology provides a divine judgement against theological polarisations, as well as grounds for theological diversity and responsibility towards ecumenical dialogue and sharing amongst diverse, yet through the Spirit's giving, communally gifted church traditions.[30]

---

[26]Chan, *Pentecostal Theology*, 97-98, 05.
[27]Ibid., 100.
[28]On the other hand, given his own argued stress on a dynamic understanding of revelation that suggests multiple meanings within biblical texts, Chan similarly proposes a restored contemporary use of *lectio divina*; see *Pentecostal Theology*, 27-28.
[29]Work, *Living and Active*, 8, 10.
[30]Ibid., 2, 9.

To conclude his project, Work centres his broad themes on two specific issues, which I will briefly focus on as relevant to this essay's concerns. The first issue is how this trinitarian-shaped ontology of Scriptures points to a hermeneutic that respects the indeterminacy of biblical texts and negotiates possible allegorical meanings. The second is that this suggests we grant interpretive space for both allegorical and authorial-centred meanings of biblical texts, arguing that diversity of textual meanings is intrinsic to a Trinitarian ecclesiology of Scripture, which arises from its Trinitarian ontology and Trinitarian soteriology.[31]

Life Formation Through the Saving Aims of Pentecostal *Lectio Divina*

Work's Trinitarian doctrine of Scripture aptly prefaces to the heart of my proposal for a Pentecostal practice of Bible reading. Briefly stated, this proposal appropriates the ancient yet enduring *lectio divina* practice to a constuctivist-narrative understanding of the early threefold Pentecostal soteriological experience of redemption, sanctification, and Spirit baptism. What results is a Pentecostal way of Bible reading that structures the reader's lifelong formative journey through these soteriological experiences. Hence, over the course of one's life-journey, these ongoing experiential processes form a Christ-shaped life in and through the key of Pentecostal spirituality.

As a needful background, I will begin by briefly describing commonly identified characteristics of the historical practice of *lectio divina*, which is most commonly associated with patristic and medieval exegesis and, hence, as a pre-critical method of Bible reading. The basic meaning of *lectio divina* is (as said at the outset) sacred (or holy) reading, which essentially comprises four parts, usually identified as: read the text (*lectio*), meditate on the text (*meditatio*), pray the text (*oratio*), and live the text (*contemplatio*). It is important to note that these four elements are not always sequential, as any of them may come to the fore at any one time. However, as a norm, this is the usual pattern.

---

[31]Ibid., 226.

Important historical developments of the *lectio divina* practice come from the 12th century Victorine and Benedictine traditions, which stressed that the primary purpose of the discipline is not spiritual illumination for its own sake *per se*, but rather to foster the Bible reader's spiritual formation.[32] Steven Chase posits that, in the Victorine tradition, the purpose of *lectio divina* as a contemplative practice is the forming of compassion within the reader, which thereby issues in charity towards the world.[33] Henri de Lubac thus notes that, in seeking out the "spiritual meaning of a text, *lectio divina* nurtures a life-long process of conversion."[34]

I will now briefly describe how *lectio divina* presumes and works through the patristic and medieval 'fourfold sense of Scripture' for the Bible reader's spiritual formation. It is commonly defined as the literal (historical), allegorical (Christological), tropological (moral), and anagogical (eschatological) senses.[35] Recognising the literal sense at the base, medieval spirituality correlated the other three senses to form the three theological virtues of faith, hope, and love. The allegorical sense thus corresponds to the virtue of faith, the tropological sense to the virtue of love, and the anagogical sense to the virtue of hope.[36] Historic Christian tradition has often correlated the four-step *lectio divina* to the fourfold Scripture sense, resulting in a spiralling and formative journey towards God-likeness. Yet again, any of the reading steps (or senses) can function at the forefront of a sequence.[37]

---

[32]Mark S. Burrows, "To Taste with the Heart: Allegory, Poetics, and the Deep Reading of Scripture," *Interpretation* (April 2002): 173.

[33]Steven Chase, *Contemplation and Compassion: The Victorine Tradition*, Traditions of Christian Spirituality Series (London, UK: Darton, Longman & Todd, Ltd., 2003), 13-14, 63-64f, 126, 148, 154.

[34]Henri De Lubac, S.J., "Spiritual Understanding," trans. by Luke O'Neill, in *The Theological Interpretation of Scripture: Classic and Contemporary Readings*, ed. Stephen E. Fowl (Oxford, UK: Blackwell Publishers, 1997): 13.

[35]Both patristic and medieval exegesis, however, demonstrate variation on prioritisation and sequence of the four senses; see Chase, *Contemplation and Compassion*, 65, footnote 3.

[36]David C. Steinmetz, "The Superiority of Pre-Critical Exegesis," in *The Theological Interpretation of Scripture: Classic and Contemporary Readings*, ed. Stephen E. Fowl (Oxford, UK: Blackwell Publishers, 1997): 29.

[37]Michael Casey, *Sacred Reading: The Ancient Art of Lectio Divina* (Liguori, MI: Triumph Books; Liguori Publications, 1996), 93.

My next step recalls the historically demonstrated affinities between the ancient practices of *lectio divina* (along with its implicitly dynamic understanding of Scriptural revelation) and practices observed within early Pentecostalism. Dale Coulter has, in fact, done so by arguing that at the centre of Pentecostal spirituality is a dynamic view of revelation. This led him to conclude that both early Pentecostals and medieval interpreters shared a common understanding that "different levels of meaning exist within the biblical texts, which necessitates an experience of the Spirit."[38]

Crucial to Coulter's argument is an earlier essay by Latin American Pentecostal theologian José Bonino, who noted similarities between medieval Bible interpretation according to the fourfold sense and early Pentecostal Bible readings, which also evidenced a multilevel hermeneutic (e.g., early issues of *The Apostolic Faith*, *The Evening Light*, and the *Church of God Evangel*).[39] Coulter thus concluded that the ancient fourfold sense of Scripture and *lectio divina* practice "provides a way of examining how Scripture functions for Pentecostals and one possible avenue for developing a Scripture principle that deeply reflects and is informed by Pentecostal sensibilities about the relation between biblical revelation and spiritual experience."[40]

Drawing again from Coulter's work, a third needful step is to establish how practioneers of the ancient practice of *lectio divina* and early Pentecostal Bible readers have correlated to their respective assumption that Scripture comprises multiple senses—i.e., multiple levels or processes of spiritual formation in the way of salvation. He notes, for instance, how early issues of *The Apostolic Faith* correlate to a multilevel hermeneutic of Bible texts the early Pentecostal threefold salvific scheme (i.e., justification, sanctification, Spirit-baptism) in consecutive meanings of Scripture, such as in studies of the three courts of the Old Testament Tabernacle—the outer court, the

---

[38] Coulter, "What Meaneth This?" *Journal of Pentecostal Theology*, 61.
[39] Ibid., 56-58; citing: José Bonino, "Changing Paradigms: A Response," in Murray A. Dempster, Byron D. Klaus, and Douglas Petersen (eds), *Globalisation of Pentecostalism: A Religion Made to Travel* (Oxford, UK: Regnum Books; Carlisle, UK: Paternoster Publishing Co., 1999), 117-119.
[40] Coulter, "What Meaneth This," *Journal of Pentecostal Theology*, 61.

holy place, and the holy of holies.⁴¹ Such early schemes again closely parallel the medieval characterisation of Christian life as a journey comprising stages of growth corresponding to levels of Scriptural meaning. In historic Christian spirituality, the most well-known of these schemes is 'Three Ways,' comprising the purgative, illuminative, and unitive ways.⁴²

Interestingly, varied assessments have observed that early North American Pentecostal multiple-stage salvific schemes implicitly retrieve patristic and medieval multi-stage soteriologies.⁴³ For the purpose of showing continuity between Pentecostal spirituality and these historic trajectories within Christian spirituality, Chan has thus suggested that the earlier Pentecostal threefold categories of salvation, sanctification, and Spirit baptism can be patterned to the Three Ways of illumination, purgation and union.⁴⁴

The final step is to integrate these respective suggestions by Coulter and Chan with Steven Land's exposition of the early Pentecostal *via salutis* (way of salvation) into the proposed Pentecostal *lectio divina* model. While Land stresses the early Pentecostal threefold blessing of salvation, sanctification, and Spirit baptism as a *via salutis* rather than an *ordo salutis,* he essentially perceives them as following a maturational-linear scheme.⁴⁵ Following through with Chan's approach to the Three Ways, I am recalibrating Land's exposition of the early Pentecostal *via salutis* according to a more constructivist understanding of the threefold Pentecostal experience.⁴⁶ Constructivism is an ancient though contemporary meta-theoretical

---

⁴¹Ibid., 58f; citing: Anonymous, "The Baptism with the Holy Ghost Foreshadowed," *The Apostolic Faith* 1, no. 4 (1906), 2; Anonymous, "Salvation According to the True Tabernacle," *The Apostolic Faith* 1, no. 10 (1907), 3.

⁴²For an introduction to the Three Ways, see: Thomas D. McGonigle, "Three Ways," in *The New Dictionary of Catholic Spirituality*, ed. Michael Downey (Collegeville, MN: Liturgical Press, 1993), 963-65.

⁴³David Bundy, "Visions of Sanctification: Themes of Orthodoxy in the Methodist, Holiness, and Pentecostal Traditions," *Wesleyan Theological Journal* 39, no. 1 (Spring 2004): 105-106, 127-135.

⁴⁴Chan, *Pentecostal Theology*, 12, 31-36f, 73-77f.

⁴⁵Land, *Pentecostal Spirituality*, 67f, 112, 114, 173, 200.

⁴⁶I have comprehensively explicated this thesis in my essay, "The *Pentecostal Triple Way*: An Ecumenical Model of the Pentecostal *Via Salutis* and Soteriological Experience," in *A Future for Holiness: Pentecostal Explorations*, ed. Lee Roy Martin (Cleveland, TN: CPT Press, 2013), 145-170.

perspective that emphasises construction of life and/or meaning through ordering and patterning processes. Constructivist psychology thus stresses that people construct meaning to their lives through discovering patterns that provide coherence to their life experiences.[47] While some ancient Christian understandings of spiritual formation followed maturational-linear schemes, others approached spiritual formation in a more constructivist manner, thus appreciating the dynamics of purgation, illumination, and union as three concurrent, repeatable, and spiralling processes leading towards spiritual and life formation.[48]

One more important element to retrieve from Land is his notion of "Pentecostal apocalyptic affections." He argues that the Pentecostal threefold blessing consistently issues in what he calls the apocalyptic affections, given that "they are constituted by the distinctive eschatological realty and vision of Pentecostal spirituality."[49] These comprise the following triad of affections—gratitude as praise-thanksgiving (issuing from redemptive experiences); the blessing of compassion as love-longing (sanctifying experiences); and courage as confidence-hope (Spirit-baptism experiences). He also suggests that these three affections fund three forms of Pentecostal prayer. The first is *prayer with words understood*, which issues from the affection of gratitude and corresponds to the blessing of regeneration. The second is *prayer without words*, which issues from the affection of compassion (and includes sighs, groans, and laughter) and corresponds to the blessing of sanctification. The third is *prayer with words not understood*, which Land associates foremost with speaking in tongues. Being an eschatological speech, tongues signifies "that the power of the end is breaking in now." Tongues speech thus issues from the affection of courage and corresponds to the blessing of Spirit-baptism. In signifying the hope of Jesus' soon coming, we may thus clarify this

---

[47]Michael J. Mahoney and Donald K. Granvold, "Constructivism and Psychotherapy," *World Psychiatry* 4 no. 2 (June 2005): 74-75.
[48]Robert Davis Hughes III, "The Holy Spirit in Christian Spirituality," in *The Blackwell Companion to Christian Spirituality*, ed. Arthur Holder (Malden, MA; Oxford UK; Victoria, Australia: Blackwell Publishing Ltd, 2005): 213, 220.
[49]Land, *Pentecostal Spirituality*, 47, 134-135, 163, 183.

third affection as "the courage of prophetic witness to the coming of the kingdom, given through experiences of Spirit baptism."⁵⁰

Therefore, Land's model of the Pentecostal *via salutis* may lead us to a Pentecostal understanding of *lectio divina* according to the following visualised scheme.

Lectio Divina	Four-fold sense	Theological aims	Pentecostal *via salutis*	Apocalyptic affections	Pentecostal prayer
Lectio	Literal	• Identity-formation via the Christian story.			
		• Identity-formation via the Pentecostal tradition.			
Meditatio	Allegorical	Faith	Redemption	Gratitude	Words understood
Oratio	Tropological	Love	Sanctification	Compassion	Without words
Contemplatio	Anagogical	Hope	Spirit-baptism	Courage	Tongues speech

This scheme also retrieves Kenneth Archer's argument that Pentecostal spirituality should function as its "central narrative convictions" for guiding Scripture reading in ways that distinctively form within readers, a distinctive identity as Pentecostals.⁵¹

The Threefold Cord That Ties Together a Pentecostal *Lectio Divina*

I shall now delineate how these contours of a Pentecostal form of *lectio divina* may help Pentecostals identify and utilise theological hermeneutics that would best foster their missiological giftedness and hence the pluralising of Pentecostalism(s) worldwide. I will do so by articulating what I shall call "The Triune Cord of Pentecostal *Lectio Divina*." I shall frame this proposal as a theological hermeneutic, which I shall describe using the metaphor of a 'threefold cord.' Ecclesiastes 4:9, 12 reads, "Two are better than one . . . but a threefold cord is not quickly broken." In good Pentecostal fashion of finding multiple meanings in the text, may I suggest an allusion to God's triune nature, and hence the Trinitarian shape of all good theology and hermeneutics. Following are three theological-hermeneutical domains inferred through this *lectio divina* model of Pentecostal theological hermeneutics.

---

⁵⁰Ibid., 139f, 154, 155, 170-171.
⁵¹Archer, *A Pentecostal Hermeneutic*, 212, 224-225.

Make Spiritual Formation the Interpretive Aim

The first cord to this proposed Pentecostal practice of Bible reading is to make spiritual formation the primary interpretive aim of Bible reading. I earlier discussed how the qualitative distinctives of Pentecostal Bible reading include relevance to daily life needs through spiritual revelation, presumed polyvalence of meaning to biblical texts, and existential identity within the biblical story-world. Yet the greater stress in classical Christian reading (and what this renewed Pentecostal appreciation towards theological diversity entails) is reading for the purpose of our life formation into the moral likeness of God shown in Christ our Lord. In the classical understanding of spiritual theology, this meant seeking out methods of Scripture reading that foster maturity along the theological virtues of faith, hope, and love. This conviction reinforces Land's thesis that Pentecostal spirituality eschatologically fuelled by our "passion for the yet coming fullness of God's kingdom" further translates the theological virtues into the three Pentecostal affections.[52] Only through this hermeneutical aim can we negotiate the interpretive diversity that signifies the many tongues of Pentecost.

Embrace the Many Tongues of Pentecost

A biblical image that contemporary Pentecostal scholarship has found helpful towards understanding the diversity found within world Pentecostalism, the Christian tradition, humanity, and hence the ecumenical promise of Pentecostalism is the "many tongues of Pentecost."[53] As the second cord, embracing Pentecost's many tongues

---

[52]Land, *Pentecostal Spirituality*, 47, 134-135, 163, 183.
[53]Pentecostal theologians who have notably worked out theological, social, and ethical implications from the basis of this theological reading include: Miroslav Volf, *Exclusion and Embrace: A Theological Exploration of Identity, Otherness, and Reconciliation* (Nashville, TN: Abingdon Press, 1996), 226-231; Amos Yong, *The Spirit Poured Out on All Flesh: Pentecostalism and the Possibility of Global Theology* (Grand Rapids, MI: Baker Academic, 2005), 196; Macchia, *Baptized in the Spirit*, 214-220; Daniela C. Augustine, *Pentecost, Hospitality, and Transfiguration: Towards a Spirit-Inspired Vision of Social Transformation* (Cleveland, TN: CPT Press, 2012), 2-3, 14-21, 30-42.

means embracing this promise as intrinsic to the giftedness of Pentecostalism towards the greater Christian tradition for the healing of fractured humanity. More specifically, this cord inculcates readers with the capacity to negotiate the reality of hermeneutical diversity evident not only in the Church Catholic, but also within global Pentecostalism. This involves a reading of the Pentecost event as the giving of ever-expanding tongues and gifts to humankind for the renewing of creation. In this sense, the many tongues of Pentecost signify the ongoing pluralization of locally gifted, interpretive communities.

Tie in the Hermeneutic of Love

Finally, this form of Pentecostal *lectio divina* suggests that we should always tie in to our theological readings of Scripture the hermeneutical cord of love—hence, a 'hermeneutic of charity.' To effectively delineate this third cord, I shall frame it within several of my previous themes—namely, the missional giftedness of global Pentecostalism, the Pentecostal dynamic view of Scripture, traditional Pentecostal assumptions about multiple levels of Bible text meanings (and thus indeterminate meanings of Scripture), and the trinitarian-ontology of Scripture. Another crucial theme I had not yet brought into this discussion is the seminal Pentecostal understanding of Spirit baptism as a baptism into God's love. I shall argue that these themes altogether deeply necessitate that we retrieve and incorporate, as a hermeneutical guide within this Pentecostal form of *lectio divina*, Augustine's hermeneutic of charity.

This suggestion reflects Work's own conclusion that Augustine's hermeneutic of love provides us a perennial guiding hermeneutic over the indeterminate meanings of Scripture. Moveover, Augustine's hermeneutic of love reflects, on one hand, his own ontological understanding of Scripture and, on the other hand, his salvific ordering of literal-to-spiritual meanings of Scripture as an *ordo salutis*, typifying the believer's journey towards union with God. Hence, Work concludes the final section of his final chapter as "The Voyage Home: Scripture's Role in Personal Salvation." Following Augustine, Work argues that it is possible to salvifically understand and order multiple meanings of Scripture, and that the key to this is a hermeneutic of charity, in which our "building up in love" becomes the aim of all Scripture reading.[54]

Crucial to Work's reflections on Augustine's hermeneutic of love is this statement from his book, *On Christian Doctrine*: "Whoever finds a lesson [in Scripture] useful to the building of charity, even though he has not said what the author may be shown to have intended in that place, has not been deceived."[55] Augustine clarifies the meaning of charity as comprising both love of God and love of one's neighbour. Hence, he argued that, if reading a text according to its literal intent fails to achieve a building up in this twofold love, then the Bible reader "does not yet understand the text as he ought."[56] He therefore concludes that a true reading of Scripture requires us to know that the aim of all Bible reading is that the Holy Spirit may form us into the love of God.[57] Work points out how for Augustine authorial intent is certainly determinative (e.g., "Anyone who understands in the Scriptures something other than that intended by them is deceived; yet Augustine nonetheless affirmed multiple meanings, insofar as they lead to right faith; hence, the building of charity."[58] Work concludes that, ultimately, justification for Augustine's hermeneutic of love lies in the true aim of Church, which is charity.[59]

Work ends his book stating that a Trinitarian ontology of Scripture inevitably accounts for the diversity of traditions and spiritualities that comprise the Church and that the diversity of biblical textual traditions and Bible translations arises from these diverse traditions and spiritualities. Moreover, both of these diversities are ultimately rooted in the plurality evoked through the perichoretic example of God as Trinity.[60] Work thus suggests it is this diversity that leads to a diversity of Bible translations, traditions of interpretation,

---

[54] Work, *Living and Active*, 304.
[55] Augustine, *On Christian Doctrine*, 36:40, in John F. Thornton and Susan B. Varenne (eds)., *Late Have I Loved Thee: Selected Writings of Saint Augustine on Love* (New York, NY: Random House, Inc.; Vintage Spiritual Classics, 2006), 85; Work, *Living and Active*, 58.
[56] Augustine, *On Christian Doctrine*, 36:40; in *Late Have I Loved Thee*, 85.
[57] Ibid., 85.
[58] Work, *Living and Active*, 58.
[59] Ibid., 311.
[60] Ibid., 233.

liturgies, and differing Scriptures; and that (fortunately) this is happening through the ongoing blossoming of ecumenical dialogue.[61] Hence, Work infers that we should appreciate our diverse approaches to Bible translations and their resultant textual differences as "together . . . constitutive of Scripture's status as the Church's Scripture."[62]

Following through with Work's ramifications of the Bible's Trinitarian ontology, I am seeking, through this construal of a Pentecostal form of *lectio divina*, to encourage Pentecostals towards an ecumenical posture that looks for resources amongst the spiritual diversities that comprise the Church Catholic, which can enrich Pentecostal tradition and spirituality. As we find theological resources that are congruent to Pentecostal spirituality, such as the ancient practice of *lectio divina*, this endeavour will deepen our identity as a distinctive spiritual tradition that allows us to better minister back to the Church Catholic our own unique gifts of the Spirit. Therefore, a hermeneutic of love, which recognises our "building up into the love of God" as an ultimate aim of Bible reading, substantiates a growing awareness in Pentecostal theology that Pentecostal experiences of Spirit baptism should be appreciated as outpourings of God's love.[63] This is a love that empowers us for mission and forms us into His moral likeness, which we declare through the Full Gospel of Christ our Saviour, Sanctifier, Spirit Baptiser, Healer, and Coming King.

Conclusion

As a caveat, I should stress that the model I have presented here stands incomplete and evokes questions that would require further explication. Among these questions would be the following: How can the suggested practice be integrated with more historical-critical approaches and hermeneutical concerns? How can the fourfold *lectio divina* sequence be more specifically practiced within the context of Pentecostal spirituality? How can the main themes and symbols characteristic of Pentecostal spirituality (including those of the broader

---

[61] Ibid., 262, 295.
[62] Ibid., 297.
[63] Macchia, *Baptized in the Spirit*, 18, 63, 258, 271; Yong, *Spirit of Love: A Trinitarian Theology of Grace* (Waco, TX: Baylor University Press, 2012), x, 3-19.

Christian tradition) be used to guide an edifying progression through the *lectio divina* sequence? Such questions indeed suggest need for further development of the proposed model. What I would further suggest as a hermeneutical control, along with the hermeneutic of charity, is that we practice a theological reading of Scripture. As earlier alluded to in the visualised scheme, by this I mean consciously letting the broad theological themes of the Christian story shape our Scripture reading. Yet this means that, if we identify ourselves within the Pentecostal theological tradition, we should also let both the Pentecostal story and the core symbols and themes that have commonly expressed that story to shape our Scripture reading.[64]

To conclude, this proposal for a Pentecostal practice of Bible reading comprising the ancient yet enduring discipline of *lectio divina* presumes that the revelational dynamism intrinsic to Pentecostal missional giftedness is an eschata-passioned multi-perspectivalism. This multi-perspectivalism affirms a plurality of potential meaning to Biblical texts, albeit hermeneutically governed through the rule of God's love that forms us into His likeness. For fueling this giftedness are the Pentecostal experiences of Spirit baptism that are birthing worldwide the 'many flaming tongues of Pentecost.'

This construal of Pentecostal Bible reading and salvific formation also suggests a salvific role that global hermeneutical pluralism serves within God's economy of cosmic salvation and, conversely, a strong soteriological doctrine of Scripture informed by Pentecostal nuances. Following the lead of Miroslav Volf, I would moreover suggest that an important pedagogical aim of this Pentecostal theological hermeneutic is to foster formation of "catholic" churches and people open to gifts from the Spirit through the pluralities of human culture. Hence, we foster "catholic" people in the truest sense of the word—i.e., those

---

[64]Two Pentecostal theologians providing relevant exploration into these trajectories are: Kenneth Archer via his notion of Pentecostal Central Narrative Convictions (212, 224-225) in Kenneth Archer, *A Pentecostal Hermeneutic*; and Wolfgang Vondey via his respective theses that the Pentecostal Full Gospel functions as the core identify-forming narrative of Pentecostal spirituality (21-24, 288-289), along with the tradition's theological symbols, Pentecost, and altar (2, 5, 10, 255-256, 281, 291, 294), in Wolfgang Vondey, *Pentecostal Theology: Living the Full Gospel* (London, UK: Bloomsbury T&T Clark, 2017).

whom the Spirit of Pentecost is forming into the likeness of the Triune God.[65]

As catholic people in the key of Pentecost growing in the likeness of the Triune fellowship, we thus grow from binary to triadic expressions of godly truth and wisdom, even as we live in a world deeply and easily fractured through binary and polarizing construals of issues, truth, and perceptions of reality. Hence, we learn that the sacred analogy of Trinity reveals that two is incomplete for divine community. There has to be a third in order to make possible the sharing and receiving of love. There also has to be a third for generating new life, new creations, new beginnings, new destinies, new dreams, new visions. Thus we appreciate the Holy Spirit as the One who stands in the middle and calls us forward into new life, new beginnings, and new meanings, which is why the Holy Spirit is the Spirit of Truth.

The Spirit is, therefore, the Love of God who leads us away from the deadening syndrome of bifurcation (i.e., the dividing into oppositions) that blinds us from seeing alternatives that can forge better paths forward. These themes point out to us how and why the Holy Spirit is the Spirit of Fellowship, for He is the one who reveals to polarised people divided along polarised meanings of the text—the third and better way of moving us forward into the future of God's new creation.

I suggest that a Pentecostal practice of *lectio divina* as I have articulated can help rightly postured people within the sanctifying presence of the Holy Spirit, who orders us into the generative wisdom of God along the way of salvation. The Spirit of Jesus thus forms us into our primal human vocation towards generating, prophesying, and making new worlds congruent to God's eschatological renewing of creation. In so doing, we labour with God for the soon coming of His kingdom, where all of His creatures receive gifted space and His blessing to "speak, sing, and dance in a multivalent chorus of

---

[65]Volf, *Exclusion and Embrace* (50-32, 129-131); in *After Our Likeness: The Church as the Image of the Trinity* (Grand Rapids, MI: William B. Eerdmans Publishing Co., 1998), Volf defines "catholic personalities" and "catholic communities" as proleptic microcosms of God's renewed creation (211-212, 276-278, 281).

tongues."⁶⁶ May we therefore foster Pentecostal spirituality throughout the earth, thus fostering the ongoing pluralities of local gifted tongues worldwide, the planting of local Pentecostal hermeneutical communities wherever new horizons emerge, and partnering with God in His mission towards the renewing of creation.

Bibliography

Albrecht, Daniel L. "Pentecostal Spirituality: Looking Through the Lens of Ritual." *PNEUMA: The Journal of the Society for Pentecostal Studies* 14. No. 2 (Fall 1992): 107-125.

Anderson, Allan H. *An Introduction to Pentecostalism: Global Charismatic Christianity.* Cambridge, UK: Cambridge University Press, 2004.

_____. *To the Ends of the Earth: Pentecostalism and the Transformation of World Christianity.* Oxford, UK: Oxford University Press, 2013.

Anonymous. "Salvation According to the True Tabernacle." *The Apostolic Faith* 1. No. 10 (1907).

Anonymous. "The Baptism with the Holy Ghost Foreshadowed." *The Apostolic Faith* 1. No. 4 (1906).

Archer, Kenneth J. *A Pentecostal Hermeneutic: Spirit, Scripture and Community.* Journal of Pentecostal Theology Supplement Series, No. 28. London, UK; New York, NY: T&T Clark International, 2004; Cleveland, TN: CPT Press, 2009.

Augustine. *On Christian Doctrine.* In *Late Have I Loved Thee: Selected Writings of Saint Augustine on Love.* Eds. John F. Thornton and Susan B. Varenne. New York, NY: Random House, Inc.; Vintage Spiritual Classics, 2006.

Augustine, Daniela C. *Pentecost, Hospitality, and Transfiguration: Towards a Spirit-inspired Vision of Social Transformation.* Cleveland, TN: CPT Press, 2012.

Bayer, Oswald. "Hermeneutical Theology." *Scottish Journal of Theology* 56. No. 2 (2003): 131-147.

Bonino, José. "Changing Paradigms: A Response." In *Globalisation of Pentecostalism: A Religion Made to Travel.* Eds. Murray A.

---

⁶⁶James K.A. Smith, *The Fall of Interpretation: Philosophical Foundations for a Creational Hermeneutic*, 2nd ed. (Grand Rapids, MI: BakerAcademic, 2012), 196-197.

Dempster, Byron D. Klaus, and Douglas Petersen, 116-126. Oxford, UK: Regnum Books; Carlisle, UK: Paternoster Publishing Co., 1999.

Bradt, Kevin M. *Story as a Way of Knowing*. Kansas City, KA: Sheed & Ward, 1997.

Bundy, David. "Visions of Sanctification: Themes of Orthodoxy in the Methodist, Holiness, and Pentecostal Traditions." *Wesleyan Theological Journal* 39. No. 1 (Spring 2004): 104-136.

Burrows, Mark S. "'To Taste with the Heart:' Allegory, Poetics, and the Deep Reading of Scripture." *Interpretation* (April 2002): 168-180.

Camery-Hoggatt, Jerry. "The Word of God from Living Voices: Orality and Literacy in the Pentecostal Tradition." *PNEUMA: The Journal of the Society for Pentecostal Studies* 27. No. 2 (Fall 2005): 225-255.

Casey, Michael. *Sacred Reading: The Ancient Art of Lectio Divina*. Liguori, MI: Triumph Books; Liguori Publications, 1996.

Chan, Simon. *Pentecostal Theology and the Christian Spiritual Tradition*. Journal of Pentecostal Theology Supplement Series, No. 21. Sheffield, UK: Sheffield Academic Press, 2000.

_____. "The Church and the Development of Doctrine." *Journal of Pentecostal Theology* 13. No. 1 (2004): 57-77.

Chase, Steven. *Contemplation and Compassion: The Victorine Tradition*. Traditions of Christian Spirituality Series. London, UK: Darton, Longman and Todd Ltd, 2003.

Coulter, Dale M. "What Meaneth This? Pentecostals and Theological Inquiry." *Journal of Pentecostal Theology* 10. No. 1 (2001): 38-64.

Davies, Andrew. "What does it Mean to Read the Bible as a Pentecostal?" *Journal of Pentecostal Theology* 18 (2009): 216-229.

Grenz, Stanley J. and John R. Franke. *Beyond Foundationalism: Shaping Theology in a Postmodern Context*. Louisville, KY: Westminster John Knox Press, 2001.

Hollenweger, Walter J. *Pentecostalism: Origins and Developments Worldwide*. Peabody, MA: Hendrickson Publishers, 1997.

Hughes III, Robert Davis. "The Holy Spirit in Christian Spirituality." In *The Blackwell Companion to Christian Spirituality*. Ed. Arthur Holder, 207-222. Malden, MA; Oxford UK; Victoria, Australia: Blackwell Publishing Ltd, 2005.

Irvin, Dale T. "Pentecostal Historiography and Global Christianity: Rethinking the Question of Origins." *PNEUMA: The Journal of the Society for Pentecostal Studies* 27, No. 1 (Spring 2005): 35-50.

Land, Steven Jack. *Pentecostal Spirituality: A Passion for the Kingdom.* Journal of Pentecostal Theology Supplement Series 1. Sheffield, UK: Sheffield Academic Press. 1993; Cleveland, TN: CPT Press, 2010.

Lubac, Henri De, S.J. "Spiritual Understanding." Trans. by Luke O'Neill. In *The Theological Interpretation of Scripture: Classic and Contemporary Readings.* Ed. Stephen E. Fowl, 3-25. Oxford, UK: Blackwell Publishers, 1997.

Macchia, Frank D. *Baptized in the Spirit: A Global Pentecostal Theology.* Grand Rapids, MI: Zondervan, 2006.

"Theology, Pentecostal." In *The New International Dictionary of Pentecostal and Charismatic Movements.* Rev Ed. Eds. Stanley M. Burgess and Eduard M. van der Mass. Grand Rapids, MI: Zondervan Publishing House, 2002.

Mahoney, Michael J. and Donald K. Granvold. "Constructivism and Psychotherapy." *World Psychiatry* 4. No. 2 (June 2005): 74-77.

McGonigle, Thomas D. "Three Ways." In *The New Dictionary of Catholic Spirituality.* Ed. Michael Downey. Collegeville, MN: Liturgical Press, 1993.

Oden, Thomas C. *Life in the Spirit. Systematic Theology.* Vol. 3 New York, NY: HarperSanFransicso; HarperCollins Publishers, 1994.

Raschke, Carl. *The Next Reformation: Why Evangelicals Must Embrace Postmodernity.* Grand Rapids, MI: Baker Academic; Baker Publishing Group, 2004.

Rice, Monte Lee. "The *Pentecostal Triple Way*: An Ecumenical Model of the Pentecostal *Via Salutis* and Soteriological Experience." In *A Future for Holiness: Pentecostal Explorations.* Ed. Lee Roy Martin, 145-170. Cleveland, TN: CPT Press, 2013.

Steinmetz, David C. "The Superiority of Pre-Critical Exegesis." In *The Theological Interpretation of Scripture: Classic and Contemporary Readings.* Ed. Stephen E. Fowl, 26-38. Oxford, UK: Blackwell Publishers, 1997.

Volf, Miroslav. *After Our Likeness: The Church as the Image of the Trinity.* Grand Rapids, MI: William B. Eerdmans Publishing Co., 1998.

_____. *Exclusion and Embrace: A Theological Exploration of Identity, Otherness, and Reconciliation.* Nashville, TN: Abingdon Press, 1996.

Vondey, Wolfgang. *Pentecostal Theology: Living the Full Gospel.* London, UK: Bloomsbury T&T Clark, 2017.

Work, Telford. *Living and Active: Scripture in the Economy of Salvation.* Grand Rapids, MI: William B. Eerdmans Publishing Co., 2002.

Yong, Amos. *Spirit of Love: A Trinitarian Theology of Grace.* Waco, TX: Baylor University Press, 2012.

_____. *The Spirit Poured Out on All Flesh: Pentecostalism and the Possibility of Global Theology.* Grand Rapids, MI: Baker Academic, 2005.

TOWARDS BECOMING A TRANSFORMATIONAL TEACHER: Teachers' Delivery Style Harmonizing with Students' Learning Styles

Weldyn Houger

In a study of transformational teaching, an understanding of teachers' delivery styles and students' learning styles is essential. In this article, pertinent literature is reviewed which helps both to develop a pedagogical framework for today's theological and biblical teacher and to "consider ways to link up with the work and ideas of others" (Wolcott, 2001, 75). Theorists, such as Lingenfelter and Lingenfelter, Pratt, Gardner, Kolb, Posner, McTighe and Wiggins, and Nisbett provide concepts and praxis for this framework while exploring various components of the teacher-learning process.

These components include the following concepts. Lingenfelter and Lingenfelter (2003) posit that the social context brings varied expectations for the role of the teacher. Pratt (1998), reviewing the broad-spectrum of teaching, discusses five pedagogical perspectives. Lynn McAlpine, Cynthia Weston, D. Berthiaume and Fairbank-Roch argue that pedagogical content integrates with the instructional materials and the physical setting. Howard Gardner (1995, 1999), a foremost expert in the field of learning styles and multiple intelligences, provides insights into learning styles which enable the teacher to transmit or transfer knowledge in an appropriate manner for the student. Kezar (2001) concurs with Gardner that students will learn and assimilate best according to their strong intelligence among multiple intelligences. Finally, Kolb's (1984) view on learning is significant for this study, as it allows for the integration of cognitive and affective learning.

The theories, concepts, and structures of these theorists and practitioners together with the relationship of the teacher's delivery style to the student's learning style will be examined in this article.

The Teacher's Delivery Style

Lois LeBar's (1995) assessment of the modern day classroom experience makes learning look negative and hopeless. She describes the learning process as the professor disseminating information and the student regurgitating it back to the professor. This assessment did not portray learning as a pleasant or memorable classroom experience (32).

In contrast, when Elizabeth Murray Morelli (2002) assesses her undergraduate classroom experience and her current classes as a professor, she describes learning as a positive encounter. She draws from her professor's classroom where the students develop into a close community of learners. Her concept of the goals of delivery styles includes: to influence the student's learning, to build a learning desire to comprehend knowledge, and to lead students into the truth (238, 242, 243). Yet, as diligently as she works to build her students into a community of learners, she acknowledges her limited influence on their character development. However, they also have other teachers that influence their lives and build character and in the process, the student experiences transformation.

What is the difference between the LeBar and Morelli scenarios? The difference lies within the teacher's delivery style. The teacher's delivery style influences whether the classroom will support learning. Although Carter and Boyle's comments are meant for the information technology world, their understanding of delivery becomes foundational for relevant delivery styles within the Bible school's context:

> Delivery of material in education is clearly important. It is apparent that students do not learn by simply being present in

a room whilst someone stands at the front and attempts to transmit information to them. . . . If we are to accept this constructivist model of education, and if students are to construct meaningful and relevant mental models of the issues and the material presented to them, then a supportive environment is clearly required. This can be problematic for teaching staff, as students will demonstrate a variety of learning styles that need to be accommodated (Carter and Boyle, 2002, 80).

Explanations of preferred teacher delivery styles vary from author to author. For example, Michener (2005) suggests that teachers intentionally "model learning behavior" and model "life's discipline" to the learners (482-483). Palmer (1998) states: "Good teaching cannot be reduced to technique; good teaching comes from the identity and integrity of the teacher" (10). He further posits that the teacher should draw the student into the subject matter. In other words, the teacher must have a repertoire of delivery styles. The following authors provide more perspectives on preferred delivery styles.

Morelli's Delivery Perspective

Morelli sees students and teachers as a community of learners who discover the content of the subject and make a commitment to understand the truth of the content. She (2002) examines Ignatius' commitment to higher education, noting that Ignatius promoted personal student-teacher relations: "the teacher must get to know the student personally so as to aid the student's moral and religious as well as intellectual development" (235). As a result, Morelli focuses her attention on the student to "educate the whole person in the areas of morals and responsibility" (241). The teacher's delivery style should not create a classroom of competitors or a fragmented class of excellent students with average students and the academic challenged students, but as Palmer (1998) says, a community of learners and collaborators of possible solutions.

Morelli (2002) also explains that her professor served as a role model of compassion and sincerity (238). She explains her professor's

Jesuit pedagogy: "a genuine love and personal care for each of our students" (238). This model influences her in her own role as professor. On the other hand, Palmer (1998) advocates for the nucleus value of education: "the core mission of education—the mission of knowing, teaching, and learning" (94). So although there is "genuine love and personal care" for the students, teaching transpires because the teacher leads the student to experience the meaning of knowledge (Kolb) and understanding (McTighe and Wiggins).

McAlpine, Weston, Berthiaume, and Fairbank-Roch's Delivery Perspective

A possible link exists between the teacher's delivery style and the actual teaching pedagogy (McAlpine, et al, 2006, 126). McAlpine, et al explain the framework for the teacher's delivery and explore the "integration of cognition and instruction," including problem solving within internal and external worlds (126). The teacher must evaluate his or her conception and performance of teaching. If the foundation of the teacher's conception for teaching rests on the amount of knowledge the teacher possesses, then his or her teaching style will follow accordingly. If the teacher possesses a particular conception of teaching, the delivery style should harmonize with the learning style of the student.

McAlpine, et al (2006) further explains about pedagogy: "pedagogical knowledge is knowledge of teaching strategies and methods in general, including references to instructional materials and physical setting" (135). Teachers must be aware of teaching strategies, methodologies, and content that work in harmony within various contexts of learning.

Interestingly, Boldt (1992) and Campbell (2002) explain that teachers must adapt to other teaching methodologies to integrate content with the lecture method. Amundsen, et al admit, "most professors have very little practice or experience with teaching methods other than traditional lecture or discussion formats . . ." (2004, 72). The need for teachers to expand their ability to implement a variety of teaching methods will become clearer in the following pages.

Ken Bain's Delivery Perspective

Ken Bain (2004) investigates seven principles and techniques that work with the lecture method:
1. The teacher creates a "natural critical learning environment."
2. The role of the teacher attracts the attention of the students and then maintains their attention.
3. The teacher begins with what the students know and then leads them into the body and framework of the discipline.
4. The teacher "seeks commitments" from the students according to the course objectives.
5. The teacher encourages students to use class material and instruction for outside assignments.
6. The teacher encourages student engagement in a similar fashion to the way scholars interact and think about the discipline.
7. The teacher "creates diverse learning experiences" (99 -116).

Bain's practical suggestions could complement any delivery style. The teacher's tone of speech should stimulate learning. The teacher should give quality explanations and involve the students in the content of the lesson and discussion (117-134).

Pratt's Delivery Perspective

From Pratt's (1998) perspective, the foundation for teaching rests on the "technical or skill-based activities of the teacher, more than on any underlying beliefs or intentionality" (37). Often times it is assumed that effective delivery styles remain the same regardless of contexts, learners or content. This assumption cannot be true because each culture demonstrates effective ways for teaching within the culture. Teachers should learn new delivery styles and appropriately use the styles. Yet, teachers should logically commit to use delivery styles that are appropriate for the students' learning style. The teacher's commitment to a diversity of approaches and perspectives of learning broadens the forte of the teacher's ability to teach in cross-ethnic situations.

Although Pratt's (1998) research reveals application for andragogy, his insights for delivery style approaches challenge the broader scope of higher education. This concept means that the teacher does not only cover content, but intentionally appropriates activities with content to bring about significant transformation. He has several good propositions regarding teaching, but the importance of his study relates to the teachers "belief about teaching and learning" (12), which engages the student with the content that results in learning.

Brookfield (1991) adds to the discussion of teacher's intentional delivery style by observation of the "teacher credibility" with the students (51). The teacher demonstrates, through personal development and experiences, how the subject's content looks in real life. This draws the students into a community of learners while the teacher informally teaches on various contradictions and complexities of life.

Johnson and Pratt's (1998) investigation examines classroom practices including the implementation of various teaching methodologies, lesson preparation, and teachers' understanding the audience's learning style. Calling their approach the "apprentice perspective" (83), Johnson and Pratt explain teaching as: "the process of enculturating learners into a specific community . . . a group of people with a common sense of identity and purpose, and clearly defined roles . . ." (43). This type of community encounter brings out the meaning of life for the student, as well as the meaning of values, behaviors, and understanding (Mezirow, 1991, 4; Mezirow, 1990. 8).

Lingenfelter and Lingenfelter's Perspective

Teaching styles vary from East to West and from teacher to teacher. Lingenfelter and Lingenfelter (2003) observe that students from the East expect their teacher to teach with authority, while the students from the West expect the teacher to be a guide and lead them to a challenge (72). Morelli (2002) and Palmer (1998) express the Western perspective. Morelli continually desires her students to enter the process of discovery of truth. This type of teaching enhances the emotional growth of the student. Palmer encourages the teacher to develop a community of learners who search for truth from content. LeBar (1995) explains it more from the perspective of the academics: "a professor who helped you understand your academic discipline . . . helped you struggle with the implications for life" (31-32).

Lingenfelter and Lingenfelter further note the dynamics of the teacher and the learner in the classroom. Similar to Pratt's delivery perspectives, the teaching style depends on the context of the learning styles. As teachers enter a specific culture, teachers "must rethink" their role within the classroom (82). First they advocate that teachers learn alongside all the learners. Second, teachers must learn their role within the new culture. Finally, they explain that teachers must be willing to surrender some of their preconceived teacher-role ideas and consent to a role that harmonizes more with the social and cultural context of the student (82-83).

No matter what the role of the teacher becomes, content should be relevant and transformational. Lingenfelter and Lingenfelter's (2003) descriptive role of the teacher gives concrete indications of "different social contexts of teaching and learning" (73). The local contexts should influence the teacher's teaching style and the type of learning that happens in the classroom.

In addition, Meyer (2002) states, "classroom environment must be established to meet the individual needs of students in each class" (258). The teacher's role pulls the students together and they collectively work, play, and plan.

While teacher-learning dynamics, teacher roles, and local contexts must be assessed, class content also must be relevant. Elyse Ashburn (2006) quotes Randy Best: "many existing colleges of education allow professors too much freedom to teach whatever they please, often ignoring research on what skills make for effective teaching" (para. 13). He further acknowledges: "relevancy is critical – that we approach this not only from the research but also from the practitioner's perspectives" (para. 13). The student brings much to the classroom. For example, the student brings his or her worldviews, beliefs, and a variety of experiences, which are relevant for the current subject matter. Teachers begin to build new knowledge and experiences upon the existing knowledge of the student.

In relating the need for building knowledge to theological teaching, Roger Erbetz's (2006) reviews *Disciplines as Frameworks for Student Learning: Teaching the Practice of the Disciplines*, edited by Tim Riordan and James. There he states that the purpose of theological teaching is to "pass on information or to enable students to develop practices and disciplines that transform their lives" (243).

Delivery style and relevancy work in tandem between the teacher and the student. Bain sums it up well:

> great teachers are not simply great speakers or discussion leaders, they are, more fundamentally, special kinds of scholars and thinkers, leading intellectual lives that focus on learning, both theirs and their students'. Their attention to the details of performance stems from a concern for the learners, and their focus is on the nature and processes of learning rather than on the performance of the instructor (2004, 134).

Lingenfelter and Lingenfelter, Morelli, and Palmer share similar perspectives on delivery styles. These delivery styles include a strong component of building a community of learners who collaborate to discover truth and then move into relevant application. Within the above discussion, however, there appears to be a missing aspect.

From this entire discussion, a picture materializes that suggests students mimic delivery styles from their teachers, and this pattern most likely affects the student's delivery style within the ministry context (the recipient). Furthermore, there is a possible lack of community learning (learning collectively) within the Asian Assemblies of God (AG) Bible school classroom.

Student's learning styles will now be examined to help complete a teaching framework for theological institutions.

Students' Learning Styles

If the teacher's delivery style does not evoke learning, has learning transpired? Shade, et al (1997) asks the question, "What is learning? (62). Their answer requires action on the part of the learner, "Learning is a process that leads to some type of action" (62). Palmer (1998) states, "What we teach will never 'take' unless it connects with the inward, living core of our student's lives, with our students' inward teachers" (31). This article considers Kolb (1984), Shade, et al (1997), Gardner (1999), and Kezar (2001) as primary theorists for this section of literature review. Other theorists, such as Banks (1995), Palmer (1998), and Nisbett (2003), will interact with the above primary theorists. These will focus on the educational concerns of students and their grasp of content.

Richard Nisbett's (2003) research provides cultural insights, educational and learning strategies, as well as practices for both Western and Asian students. He observes and examines the students' backgrounds, worldview, people relationships, objects, religion, and environment. Nisbett's theory stresses the significance of harmony and collectivism within the Asian cultures, whereas the western cultures emphasize individualism, logic, and categories (i.e. systematic theology, leadership, individual testing, etc).

Gardner (1999) emphasizes the multiple intelligences of the student, and Banks (1995) highlights the importance of academic transformation: the desired outcome. Nisbett and Gardner focus on students, while Banks focuses on the academics.

Palmer's (1998) thoughts and perspective tie these concepts together. Palmer, as already noted, promotes community learning. This concept speaks to the need or interest of students. At the same time, community learning connects content to the students' background, previous knowledge and intelligence as they collectively discover the academic content. The teacher harmonizes the educative body of content with appropriate learning styles. (30-31).

McTighe and Wiggins (2004) aim for transferable understanding. The presentation of content in harmony with the student's intelligence produces greater transferable understanding including transformation. Further, their theory can possibly harmonize with the principles of contextualization (Hesselgrave, 1991).

Learning theorist Kezar (2001) assists and encourages educators to use Multiple Intelligences (MI). She promotes students practicing the handling of truth, and she applies content understanding according to the students' capability and intelligence. The highlight of her theory rests in the area of assessments.

Kolb's learning theory explains that "people do learning from their experience, and the results of that learning can be reliably assessed and certified for college credit" (1984, 3). Kolb's view on experiential learning does not discount cognitive learning, but encourages the integration of experiences with cognitive learning. The learner develops a lifelong process of learning. Experiential learning includes practical methods of "apprenticeships, internships, work/study programs, cooperative education, studio arts, laboratory studies, and field projects" (Kolb, 1984, 5).

The teacher must come back to the question of Shade et al (1997), "What is learning?" Their answer is: "Through the process of learning, people make changes in our knowledge base and memory storage by accumulating facts; developing and enlarging their concepts and ideas about life; and creating entirely new ideas, attitudes, beliefs, models, images, or patterns" (62). The way teachers teach and students perceive knowledge can be two different realities. Howard Gardner helps the teacher through his observations of Multiple Intelligences (MI).

Howard Gardner's Learning Theory

An essential review on Gardner's (1999) learning theory will help any teacher on the educational spectrum of learning. His conceptual thinking allows teachers to be creative with students. The teacher observes the intelligence and creative abilities of the student. As the teacher synchronizes and facilitates the lesson's content with the student's intelligence, the student experiences an increase of learning and transformation. Consequently, the student begins to experience an unveiling of the truth or content. Banks (1995) not only considers the paradigms and themes of present knowledge, but he posits that in order for knowledge to be transformative, the students should challenge the present knowledge and observe if any other stream of knowledge emerges. Possibly a new concept or explanation will emerge that will transform the life of the student.

In the early 1980's Gardner's original seven intelligences (naturalist has since been added) provided significant educational guides for teachers to understand students from multiple educational platforms. Another intelligence emerges in Campbell's investigation on intelligences. Campbell notes, "Gardner admits the possibility of spiritual intelligence" (2000, 32), a theory that has gained some recognition.

The MI (1999) theory suggests three pragmatic concepts for teachers to implement in the classroom (186). These concepts assist the teacher to know the learning styles of the student, and for the student to demonstrate his/her intelligences.

The first pragmatic concept to "inculcate understanding," is "powerful points of entry" (186). For example, the teacher could begin class with a relevant or familiar social or cultural topic, local news story, cultural fable, or cultural activity that introduces the lesson's content. As the teacher develops the point of entry activity the teacher connects new subject matter with already known knowledge. Three learning aspects come to light in this pragmatic concept: 1) The student associates new content with previous content, which has a greater chance of being remembered or further developed or implemented; 2) students' attention span becomes greater and allows cognitive learning to become more usable; 3) students become involved in the content, thus the classroom becomes learning-centered.

The second pragmatic concept focuses on the usage of "apt analogies" (1999, 187). New knowledge becomes difficult to introduce when a student does not demonstrate previous knowledge. Usage of cultural proverbs and analogies to introduce a new piece of knowledge becomes helpful. For example, an Asian AG Bible schoolteacher could introduce a theological concept with a quote from a well-known cultural proverb or analogy.

The third pragmatic concept highlights the provision of "multiple representation of central or core ideas of the topic" (1999, 187). For example, the teacher may tell a story, show a video clip (from within their culture), demonstrate a project or a special object to represent the core idea of the lesson. The students' involvement engages them in the content and encourages the teacher to look for practical application for the students' ministry context. The learner not only hears the idea, or sees the idea, but also possibly handles the idea.

The significance of these ideas becomes foundational for the teacher to lead the student to be interactive with the content and into experiential learning and application. Furthermore, the student discovers, creates, contextualizes, and applies methods in effective ways within the recipient's context. Learning happens when unveiled truth or content becomes practical and usable in another context.

According to Gardner, MI "seeks to create innovative learning environments" for the students (213). These multiple intelligences provide a platform for teachers to know the uniqueness of their students and to present knowledge that associates with the students' intelligence level.

Kezar's Response to Gardner and Perspective

Andrianna Kezar (2001) reviews implications of the multiple intelligence theory and the significance of this study, especially the subject of learner styles. Kezar expresses amazement at the lack of significant impact of Gardner's multiple intelligences on higher education (141). Kezar concurs with Gardner that intelligences are not only found in linguistics and logic, but also through spatial, music, naturalist, kinesthetic, interpersonal, and intrapersonal intelligences (2001, 143). Kezar further notes, "all individuals have natural talents that could be refined in higher education" (147). Often the evident perception among educators is to find the logical and linguistic talents to have the advantage over the other intelligences.

As it relates to the present trends in higher education, Kezar (2001) constructs a useful platform for the multiple intelligences theory, with three important implications (147). The first implication stresses: "all individuals have natural talents that could be refined in higher education." If the MI theory finds a place in higher education, Kezar acknowledges, it could accommodate all personalities of various talents. Kezar further suggests that schools could move away from multiple-choice exams and possibly modify the exams that allow the students to illustrate their competence (148).

A second implication deals with "diverse learning needs." Kezar indicates this idea as the "greatest implication for higher education" (148). Kezar's apparent implication finds that faculty "might consider teaching their courses/subject matter through the multiple intelligences" (148). Kezar further encourages the teacher to spend quality time with the student to observe the student's intelligence (148). She encourages teachers to implement the MI theory and lead the student into experiential and interactive learning. Moreover, understanding of content leads students to engage in real working contexts (Kezar, 2001, 148).

Kezar's (2001) third implication emphasizes "accountability" (150). Kezar observes that what the institution's mission statements postulate often transpires differently in the classroom. How does this relate to learning styles? She states, most "mission statements discuss the importance of understanding oneself (intrapersonal intelligence), leadership development (interpersonal intelligence), appreciation and competence in the arts (musical, kinesthetic and spatial intelligences) . . ." (150). Teachers must demonstrate accountability to the institution's mission statement but they must also establish how the student discovers new truth or content through their learning styles and intelligences. Moreover, the student needs to clearly connect the bridge between the mission of the school and the reason for their education, which should result in experiential learning and transformation.

David Kolb's Experiential Learning Theory

Kolb (1984) views humankind as "learning species" (1) who have the abilities to react to the physical and social worlds around them. Another skill for these "learning species" lies in the ability to create and shape their world (1). He further explains, "people do learn from their experiences" (3). Kolb's theory does not provide an alternative to the rationalism and behaviorism learning models, but it supplies concrete and lasting insights into learning (1984, 3). This theory pictures "a holistic integrative perspective on learning that combines experience, perception, cognition, and behavior" (21) and provides a platform for lifelong learning that is "soundly based in intellectual traditions of social psychology, philosophy, and cognitive psychology" (1984, 3-4). Finally, the theory strengthens "the critical linkages among education, work, and personal development" (4). The teacher taps into each aspect of the student and links it with essential and relevant knowledge.

Kolb compares rationalist, cognitive, and behaviorist learning theories as "acquisition, manipulation, and recall of abstract symbols, . . . that deny any role for consciousness and subjective experience in the learning process" (20). Kolb acknowledges and builds upon the works of Dewey, Lewin, and Piaget, as they relate to experientially learning. From their theories and identifiable experiential learning characteristics emerges a possible central word for experiential learning: a "process." The following show the four defining and foundational characteristics of experiential learning:

1. The process of learning finds expression in "adaptation and learning as opposed to content and outcomes" (39).
2. "Knowledge is a transformation process being continuously created and recreated, not an independent entity to be acquired or transmitted" (39).
3. Learning reveals the transformative action "in both its objective and subjective forms" (39).
4. In order for learning to be understood, the nature of knowledge needs to be understood. (39).

Kolb advocates that when learners confront new content, attitudes, and skills, the teacher must know the four modes of learning for the experiential learner. The student wants to experience effective learning, but they must have experiences that effectively implement content, attitude, and skills. The four modes of experiential learning can be described as: (a) concrete experience abilities, (b) reflective observation abilities, (c) abstract conceptualization abilities, and (d) active experimentation abilities" (30). These modes of learning assist the learner to implement and integrate knowledge with their observations and arrange their theories into a format that will help them solve problems or formulate answers for all types of decisions (1984, 30).

Kolb's definition of learning finds expression in "the process whereby knowledge emerges through the transformation of experience. Knowledge results from the combination of grasping experience and transforming it" (41). Furthermore, he describes the basic forms of knowledge in the terms of "divergent," "assimilative," "convergent," and "accommodative" (42). He clarifies that these building blocks assist in the development of higher levels of knowledge (42). In addition, two fundamental forms of action materialize on the part of the learner: (a) the student literally or figuratively grasps a portion of the experience, and (b) the student experiences transformation.

According to Kolb, a specific weakness emerges within higher education including higher theological and biblical education, which is the "failure to recognize and explicitly provide for the differences in learning styles that are characteristic of both individual and subject matters" (196). Kolb observes that educators have not sufficiently provided "alternative learning methods . . . based on the persons' learning style" (197). Kolb's comment is true for theological and biblical institutions. In addition, Kolb acknowledges a lack of sufficient research of the learning style and the subject matter in conjunction with and reliant on effective teaching methods (197).

A noteworthy factor for successful learning relates to the learning environment. Kolb takes the four modes of learning and breaks down what the teacher must do to make learning effective for the learner:

1. "Concrete experience": the teacher needs to make "personalized feedback," behave as friendly helpers, and provide "activities oriented toward applying skills to real-life problems" (200).
2. "Reflective" experiences: "teachers providing expert interpretations and guiding or limiting discussions, output being judged by external criteria of field or discipline, and lecturing" (200).
3. "Abstract conceptualization": students favor "case studies, thinking alone, and theory readings" (200).
4. "Active-experimentation": "small-group discussions, projects, peer feedback, homework problems, the teacher behaving as a model of the profession . . . and activities designed to apply skills to practical problems" (200).

Experiential learning "is a sophisticated, integrated process of learning" (225). The significance of this learning theory is that it can "interface between knowledge" and various quandaries of everyday life including becoming a contributing participant within society (225).

In summary, a cyclical picture or a continuous process develops. The student looks for the meaning of the content through the experiences. These experiences broaden the platform for new knowledge. Experience leads to meaning. Meaning leads to application and contribution to society. Contribution leads to a new experience and further transformation.

Shade, Kelly, and Oberg's Learning Perspective

Shade, Kelly, and Oberg's (1997) perspective provides understanding for the learning orientation of the student. What the teacher deems as reality and what the students deems as reality are different and unique. According to Shade et al, the students' worldview opens to "particular ways of perceiving, thinking and acting to meet the demands of their environment" (10). If each student functions this way, the student's ways of perception, thinking, and acting challenge the delivery style. A further challenge is for the teacher to continually demonstrate the ability and necessity to be a constant learner of student cultures (18).

Their discussion unfolds insights and perceptions that create ways to work along side with the student's learning process. They emphasize that the learning process is a key ingredient for the student. In their discussion, they discovered several ways that the learning process unfolds. These learning processes begin with the performance of a task. In addition, learning transpires through listening. Learning emerges through formulas and experiments, and learning manifests itself through specific experiences or through visual senses and simple observations (62-63).

Shade et al further explain the concepts of "learning styles" based on the student's preferred orientation to learning in environmental characteristics (64). Much of what the student grasps depends on his or her perception of seeing the whole picture before knowing the parts or knowing the parts before seeing the whole (65-66). Further, Shade et al realize that culture influences the style of learning (69). They expose three different meanings for learning styles:

1. "preferred orientation" – this deals with environment factors that help facilitate learning (64);
2. "students take responsibility for their own learning" depending on their "goals, needs, and interests" (64);
3. "resource management" indicates the approach the student takes to make the student "appear most competent" (65).

This perspective reveals that the center of learning must be the students. Student-centered education keeps relevancy and contextualization of content appropriate for the student's context (112-113).

Not only should teachers consider the student's identity, but should consider the origin of the student (ethnicity or student's context of community). If a student's ethnicity is slightly different than the rest of the class, the stress or anxiety level rises for the student. Shade et al suggest that until the teacher addresses the anxiety concern, learning cannot happen. The authors specifically stress that learners should "feel a sense of belonging" (99). And, if students cannot express a sense of belonging, "they cannot use their energies to learn" (99). As these learners form community, the students' individual cultures, languages, behavioral patterns, values, and worldview influences impact the formation of community and hopefully the students experience harmony. Shade et al acknowledge, "a learning community that is culturally inclusive must be led by a teacher who is warm and supportive" (45).

Students, according to Shade et al discover their role in the community and begin to accept the "concepts of cooperation and self responsibility" (90). Various organizational tasks and responsibilities help maintain the classroom order (90). This type of organization builds "feelings of pride, dignity, honor, trust, and reliability" (90). This type of community / classroom design promotes a healthy learning environment.

Shade et al describe the act of learning: "the teacher of culturally diverse students becomes a cultural liaison and has the responsibility for developing a connection between the culture of the students and the culture of the school" (19). The teacher needs to make sure the student will reproduce knowledge contextually, integrate into society, and contribute to the community. In other words, the teacher uses the cultural characteristics and background of the student to bridge the gap of the known with a new level of knowledge competencies (19). From this observation, cultural views, student thinking patterns, observations, and real life applications better enhance the transference of usable knowledge.

Mezirow's Learning Theory

Mezirow (1991) develops the transformation theory and centers the research on meaning. Although this theory targets adult learners, Mezirow expresses his theory and purpose of learning as the "perspective transformation" theory (167). Furthermore, Mezirow searches for an illumination of "universal conditions and rules that are implicit in linguistic competence or human development" (xii – xiii). He clarifies the learning structure of the learner. Furthermore, he examines how learning transforms the learner through "frames of references," which means how experiences are viewed and interpreted (page xiii). From these experiences, meanings emerge and transformation within the learner occurs. As the experiences and knowledge come together, the learners interpret the meaning of knowledge. Knowledge begins to shape "their life, their actions, their contentment and emotional well-being, and their performance" (xiii). Teachers should give ample opportunity for students to experiment with knowledge until it becomes an essential quality and component within the student's life.

Mezirow indicates, "we improve our ability to anticipate reality by developing and refining our meaning schemes and perspectives so that we may use them more effectively to differentiate and integrate experience" (146). Teachers should aim to integrate the reality issues of the students' experiences with the explanation and perspective of subject content followed by classroom discussion and reflection.

Mezirow's theory denotes that students move from one level of content and understanding through vital experiences, to another level of understanding, meanings, and thoughts. The student experiences transformation of thought, practices, and application through the educational process. New knowledge builds upon previous knowledge, paradigms shift, new affective components challenge the student's present affective domain, and student's current skills broaden to more efficient and effective skills (167).

In conclusion, Kolb, Gardner, Kezar, Mezirow and Shade et al., agree that teachers should allocate more time to understand the learning styles of students. When the teacher is a transformational agent there will be students who are transformed. Consequently, teachers' delivery styles must harmonize with students' learning styles.

References

Ashburn, Elyse (2006). A Dallas banker rethinks teacher education. *The Chronicle of Higher Education, 52* (46), 2-3. http://chronicle.com/weekly/v52/i46/46a02301. html (accessed June 6, 2007).

Bain, Ken (2004). *What the Best College Teachers Do.* Cambridge, MA: Harvard University Press.

Banks, James A. (1995). Multicultural Education and Curriculum Transformation. *The Journal of Negro Education, 64* (4), 390-400. from Jstor (accessed January 1, 2008).

Boldt, Arnold. (1998). The Transmission Perspective: Effective Delivery of Content. In Daniel D. Pratt & Associates (Eds.), *Five Perspectives on Teaching in Adult and Higher Education*, (pp. 57-82). Malabar: Fl: Krieger.

Brookfield, Stephen. (1991). Grounding Teaching Learning. In Michael W. Galbraith (Ed.), *Facilitating Adult Learning: A Transactional Process* (pp. 33-56). Malabar, FL: Krieger.

Campbell, Marla J. (2000). An Experiential Learning Approach to Faculty Training in Asia Pacific Education. *Dissertation Abstract International*, 61(04), (UMI No. 99734144).

Carter, Janet, & Boyle, Roger. (2002). Teaching Delivery Issues – Lessons for Computer Science. *Journal of Information Technology Education, 1* (2), 77-89. http://www.g oogle.com/search?q=Teaching+Delivery+Issues+-+++Lessons+from+Computer+ Science&ie=utf-8&oe=utf-&&aq=t&rls=org.mozilla:e n-US:official&client=firef ox-a (accessed February 13, 2009).

Dewey, John. (1938). *Experience and Education.* New York: Touchstone.

Ebertz, Roger P. (2006). [Review of the book, Disciplines as Frameworks for Student Learning: Teaching the Practice of the Disciplines]. *Teaching Theology and Religion, 9* (4). 243-243. Academic Search Premier (accessed June 3, 2008).

Gardner, Howard. (1995). Reflections on Multiple Intelligences. *Phi Delta Kappan 77*(3), 1-9. Academic Search Premier (accessed October 27, 2007).

_____. (1999). *The Disciplined Mind: What All Students Should Understand.* New York: Simon and Schuster.

Johnson, Janice, & Pratt, Daniel D. (1998). The Apprenticeship Perspective: Modeling Ways of Being. In Daniel D. Pratt and Associates, (Eds.), *Five Perspectives on Teaching in Adult and Higher Education* (pp. 83-103). Malabar: Fl: Krieger.

Kezar, Adrianna (2001). Theory of Multiple Intelligences Implications for Higher Education. *Innovative Higher Education, 26*(2), 141-154. Academic Search Premier (accessed November 16, 2007).

Kolb, David. (1984). *Experiential Learning.* Englewood Cliffs, NJ: Prentice-Hall.

LeBar, Lois E. (1995). *Education that is Christian.* Colorado Springs, CO: Cook Communications.

Lingenfelter, Judith E., & Lingenfelter, Sherwood G. (2003). *Teaching Cross-Culturally: An Incarnational Model for Learning and Teaching.* Grand Rapids, MI: Baker Academic.

Maxwell. (1996). *Qualitative Research Design: An Interactive Approach.* Thousand Oaks, CA: SAGE Publication, Inc.

McAlpine, Lynn, & Ralph Harris. (1999). Lessons Learned: Faculty Developer and Engineer Working as Faculty Development Colleagues. *International Journal of Academic Development, 4* (1), 11-17. Academic Search Premier (accessed June 8, 2008).

McAlpine, Lynn, Weston, Cynthia, Berthiaume, D., & Fairbank-Roch, G. (2006). How Do Instructors Explain Their Thinking When Planning and Teaching? *Higher Education. 51* (1), 125-155. Wilson Select Plus (accessed September 27, 2009).

McTighe, Jay, & Wiggins, Grant. (2004). *Understanding by Design: Professional Development Workbook.* Alexandria, VA: Association for Supervision and Curriculum Development.

Meyer, Arlin G. (2002). Teaching Literature as Mediation: A Christian Practice. In Migliazzo, Arlin C (Ed.), *Teaching as an Act of Faith: Theory and Practice in Church-Related Higher Education* (pp. 253-276). New York: Fordham University Press.

Mezirow, Jack. (1990). How Critical Reflection Triggers Transformative Learning. In J. Mezirow and Associates (Eds.), *Fostering Critical Reflection in Adulthood* (pp. 1-20). San Francisco: Jossey-Bass.

Michener, Ronald T. (2005). Missionary "Teaching" in a Postmodern Context. *Evangelical Mission Quarterly. 41*(4), 482-487.

Morelli, Elizabeth Murray. (2002). An Ignatian Approach to Teaching Philosophy. In Arlin C. Migliazzo (Ed.), *Teaching as an Act of Faith: Theory and Practice in Church-Related Higher Education* (pp. 233-252). New York: Fordham University Press.

Nisbett, Richard E. (2003). *The Geography of Thought: How Asians and Westerners Think Differently – and Why*. Boston: Nicholas Bealey.

Palmer, Parker J. (1998). *The Courage to Teach: Exploring the Inner Landscape of a Teacher's Life*. San Francisco: Jossey-Bass.

Pratt, Daniel D. (1998a). Alternative Frames of Understanding: Introduction to Five Perspectives. In Daniel D. Pratt & Associates (Eds.), *Five Perspectives of Teaching in Adult and Higher Education* (pp. 33-53). Malabar, FL: Krieger.

_____. (1998b). Analytical Tools: Epistemic, Normative, and Procedural beliefs. In Daniel D. Pratt & Associates (Eds.), *Five Perspectives of Teaching in Adult and Higher Education* (pp. 203-216). Malabar, FL: Krieger.

_____. (1998c). The Research Lens: A General Model of Teaching. In Daniel D. Pratt (Ed.), *Five Perspectives of Teaching in Adult and Higher Education* (pp. 3-14). Malabar, FL: Krieger.

Shade, Barbara J., Kelly, Cynthia, & Oberg, Mary. (1997). *Creating Culturally Responsive Classrooms*. Washington, DC: American Psychological Association.

Smith, Mark. (2008). *Howard Gardner, Multiple Intelligences and Education*. http://www.infed.org/thinkers/gardner.htm#multiple_intelligences (accessed February 15, 2009).

Wolcott. (2001). *Writing up Qualitative Research.* (2nd ed.). Thousand Oaks, CA: SAGE Publication, Inc.

HOW CULTURAL ANTHROPOLOGY INFORMS AND ENHANCES DOING THEOLOGY AND THEOLOGICAL EDUCATION IN ASIA

Dave Johnson

At the Asia Theological Association's (ATA) Consultation in Malang, Indonesia, in July, 2017, it was noted in a plenary session that Asian theologians often do not know how to exegete culture. Over the years in which I have served as the managing editor of the *Asian Journal of Pentecostal Studies*,[1] I have repeatedly challenged our authors to think through what they have written within the Asian context. True biblical theology[2] is never separated from the human situation.

This paper will address the issue of exegeting culture, using the sermons of Paul to the Jews of Pisidian Antioch (Acts 13:13-47) and the Greeks on Mars Hill (Acts 17: 22-31).[3] This will demonstrate how cultural anthropology can enhance doing theology and theological training in Asia so that the challenges of a mostly western theological tradition can be overcome.

---

[1] The Journal can be found at www.aptspress.org.
[2] I use the term biblical theology here in the broader sense of any type of theologizing that is consistent with Scripture.
[3] I agree with Flemming that these passages present excellent case studies in contextualization. Dean Flemming, *Contextualization in the New Testament: Patterns for Theology and Mission* (Downer's Grove, IL: Inter-Varsity Press, 2005), 57.

To do this, understanding the nature of culture is important. Legions of definitions abound, but Hiebert's concise definition is sufficient here. Hiebert maintains that culture is "the more or less integrated systems of ideas, feelings, and values and their associated patterns of behavior and products shared by a group of people who organize and regulate what they think, feel, and do."[4] Due to space limitations, however, only the concept of worldview, which, according to Charles Kraft, lies at the heart of any culture, can be examined here.[5]

Worldview

Kraft explains the place of worldview within culture:

Culture consists of two levels: the surface behavior level and the deep worldview level. At the core of culture and, therefore, at the very heart of all human life, lies the structuring of the base assumptions, values and allegiances in terms of which people interpret [the world] and behave. These assumptions, values and allegiances we call worldview.[6]

Andrew Walls states that "worldviews are the mental maps of the universe that contain what we know, or think we know, about the universe, how it operates, and about our own place in it. We use these maps to navigate our way through daily life."[7]

While the issue of worldview is too broad to discuss in detail here, it can be stated that a society's values and behaviors are formed by its worldview. In other words, worldview drives culture. Walls goes on to say that the concept of worldview goes beyond the phenomenal world of what can be heard, touched and seen, to include the sphere of

---

[4]Paul Hiebert, *Anthropological Insights for Missionaries* (Grand Rapids: Baker Book House, 1985), 30.

[5]Charles, Kraft, *Christianity in Culture: A Study in Dynamic Biblical Theologizing in Cross Cultural* Perspective (Maryknoll, NY: Orbis Books, 1979), 53.

[6]Charles H. Kraft, *Anthropology for Christian* Witness (Maryknoll, NY: Orbis Books, 1996), 11.

[7]Andrew Walls, *Crossing Cultural Frontiers: Studies in the History of World Christianity*, (Maryknoll, NY: Orbis Books, 2017), 35.

religion.⁸ According to Hiebert, worldview is the vehicle through which people interpret and explain reality.⁹ For those in ministry, worldview transformation is critical for bringing people to maturity in Christ.

One of the critical issues for theological education in an Asian context is the fact that all Asian societies are deeply rooted in an animistic worldview. This is true even though most Asians are followers of one of the world's formal religions: Hinduism and Buddhism in all of their varieties, Islam, Christianity, Shintoism, Chinese ethnic religions such as Daoism or smaller religions such as Jainism and Sikhism. Noted Islamic scholar Phil Parshall observed that 70% of all Muslims practice folk Islam.[10] While actual data is hard to come by, observation and anecdotal evidence regarding the level of animism embedded in the other religious cultures would suggest a similar situation.

In the following selected texts, Paul's approach to teaching the gospel to two diverse worldviews is explored. His exegesis of both cultures results in a dramatically different gospel presentation to each audience.

The Jewish Monotheistic Worldview (Acts 13:13-41)

In the synagogue at Pisidian Antioch, Paul spoke to diaspora Jews and, most likely, Gentiles who were drawn to monotheism and were known as God-fearers. He begins with a recitation of Israelite history in order to document the Messianic claims of Christ. As he does so, he demonstrates an outstanding ability to exegete Jewish culture.

For the Jews, there was one God whose existence was assumed. None of the biblical writers, including Paul, felt the need to prove God's existence. Furthermore, God's power was absolute and he demonstrated that power throughout their history, as Paul relates here. He does not say, because he does not need to, that God displayed his power over the gods of Egypt (Ex. 12:12) and also over the gods of the

---

⁸Walls, 35.
⁹Paul Hiebert, *Cultural Anthropology*, 2nd ed. (Grand Rapids: Baker Book House, 1983), 357.
[10]Phil Parshall, *Bridges to Islam* (Grand Rapids: Baker Book House, 1983), 16.

nations they conquered in the desert and in the Promised Land. Paul's listeners here would have well understood his reference to God's power over the other so-called gods because of their worldview assumptions. It is possible that here Paul is also making an oblique reference to the inferior power of the gods of the Greek pantheon, especially since there were Greek God-fearers in attendance (13:16). He may also be referring to folk Judaism,[11] but neither of these are the thrust of his argument.

There is more to the Jewish worldview here, however, than God's power. Another Jewish worldview assumption that runs through Paul's message is God's immutability. Throughout Israel's history, God's character was constant and consistent. He was their patron, protector and provider. Again, this is in stark contrast to the polytheistic[12] worldview of the Jews' Gentile neighbors, whose gods were capricious and had to be constantly appeased by sacrifice—a practice well known to Asians today for the same reason. One can note that where the Scriptures correspond to a culture's worldview, less instruction is needed.

Second, Paul speaks to a more diverse culture, the Greeks on Mar's Hill.

The Ancient Greek Worldview

Here, Paul is speaking to the intellectuals of Athens, the philosophers who spent their days endlessly debating philosophy. Both Stoics and Epicureans were likely in attendance and the meeting took place literally under the shadow of the Acropolis, where the Greek pantheon of gods had one of their major temples. In his message, he begins with an allusion to Greek history, then goes on to creation, and as with the Jews in Pisidian Antioch, ends with the death and resurrection of Christ. Again, Paul demonstrates a marvelous grasp of

---

[11]The story of Bar-Jesus in Acts 13:1-8 gives an example of the folk Judaism practiced at the time.

[12]In relationship to worldview, the terms polytheistic and animistic are virtually interchangeable, except that in polytheism the spirit beings involved are normally thought of as gods and in animism they are thought of as either gods or spirits. Their functions are virtually the same.

the cultural themes that impact the Greeks' understanding of his message.

In contrast to the monotheistic Jews, the ancient Greeks worshiped a cafeteria of gods,[13] none of whom were held to be all-powerful. Athens, for all of its humanistic philosophy, had a legion of temples, statues and altars for every kind of purpose, which Stott described as "a veritable forest of idols."[14] One Roman satirist noted that, in Athens, "it was easier to find a god than a man."[15] Some of the gods worshiped there were Zeus, Apollo, Aphrodite, Hermes, the Muses, Artemis, Asclepius, Poseidon, Serapis and many others. Arnold notes that "the Church fathers strongly believed that Satan himself animated these gods and goddesses with his powers of darkness. Their demonic interpretation of these religions originated, in part, with the apostle Paul,"[16] (see Deut. 32:17; I Cor. 10:20).

All of this reflects a supernatural, animistic worldview, which Julie Ma defines as

> [A] belief in personal spirits and impersonal spiritual forces. Animists also perceive that the spirits and forces have power over human affairs. People who have experienced such spiritual power and influence constantly seek its help to meet various daily human needs such as healing, success, and decisions for the future. They attempt to manipulate the power of the spirits for the [sic] favourable future.[17]

None of the Greek gods called for exclusive worship, nor did they demand moral behavior. With the exception of Allah in Islam, the gods of Asia are much the same way. Among the

---

[13] Larry Hurtado, *Destroyer of the Gods: Early Christian Distinctiveness in the Roman World* (Waco, TX: Baylor University Press, 2016), Kindle loc 838-9.
[14] Stott, 277.
[15] Ibid.
[16] Clinton Arnold, *Powers of Darkness: Principalities & Powers in Paul's Letters* (Downer's Grove, IL: Inter-Varsity Press, 1992), 45. Clinton has done other good work in the area of animism in the background of the NT and I have noted these works in the bibliography.
[17] Julie C. Ma, "Animism and Pentecostalism" in *Encyclopedia of Pentecostal and Charismatic Christianity* (New York: Routledge, 2006), 26-27, quoted in Wonsuk and Julie Ma, *Mission in the Spirit: Toward a Pentecostal-Charismatic Missiology* (Oxford, UK: Regnum Books International, 2010), 108.

Chinese, for example, many practice Taoism, Confucianism and Buddhism, along with animism, without noting any distinctions between them.

Speaking to people who were convinced that a variety of gods controlled the sky, the weather and virtually every other aspect of life, Paul demonstrates great familiarity with their worldview, no doubt because he had grown up in Tarsus, a cosmopolitan Gentile city. As Walls expressed it above, he could read their mental maps. He was also obviously familiar with their literature and history.[18]

Worldview Assumptions

Kraft notes that people in various cultures reach different conclusions regarding their worldview because they start from different assumptions.[19] These assumptions are seldom critically evaluated unless they are challenged.

The Jews

Here, Paul could go directly to the Scriptures because the Jews assumed the divine authority of the Old Testament (OT). They also assumed the reality of Messianic prophecy (13:32-36), although they would not have ascribed the fulfillment to Jesus.

The Athenians

Paul's reference to the Altar to the Unknown God draws on an ancient tradition that an unknown god stopped a plague that was ravaging the Greeks.[20] As Ma mentions above, one of the assumptions of animism is that supernatural power can be used for curing disease.

---

[18] For an excellent discussion on Paul's use of Greek literature, see Craig S. Keener, *Acts: An Exegetical Commentary,* vol. 3 (Grand Rapids: Baker Academic, 2014), 2653-2664.

[19] Kraft, *Christianity in Culture,* 57.

[20] In his excellent book, *Eternity in Their Hearts,* Rev. ed., (Ventura, CA: Regal Books, 1981), 9-25, Don Richardson explains the background of the altar to the Unknown God. Keener also mentions this, (Keener, 2657).

Paul's highlighting of this unknown God has another purpose, however. This unknown God serves as Paul's illustration of the difference between Athenian cultural assumptions and the truth of Scripture. Paul highlights this in his teaching precisely because this is where worldview change must begin.

At the same time, Paul honors Athenian culture through another reference to their context. His reference to "in him we live and move and have our being," (17:28) may be drawn from Greek literature,[21] but it reveals one of the assumptions of animism that all of life is spiritual and connected to the supernatural.[22] Van Rheenen notes that animists contend that there are personal spirit beings and impersonal forces everywhere" that shape what happens in the world.[23] This connection between the divine and the human is also seen in v. 28. Here, Keener notes that the Greeks commonly believed that Zeus or one of the other deities were the progenitors of humanity.[24]

In all of these cases, Paul's keen understanding of this worldview allowed him to build bridges between the worldview of both the Jews and the Greeks while impacting their cultural assumptions with a God centered worldview focused on "man whom he has appointed" (v31), Jesus the Christ.

Worldview Transformation

My premise here, following Kraft, is that God, who himself is above culture, works through it to achieve his purposes.[25] In teaching and preaching the call for worldview transformation, which is inherent in the gospel itself, demands that allegiance be given only to the God of the Bible. Kraft notes that "when people become Christians, they make certain changes in their deep-level worldview assumptions, values, and allegiances."[26] In other words, their mental maps are redrawn. The challenge of theological training in both Asia and the

---

[21]Keener, 2657-8.
[22]Kevin Hovey (class lecture, Asia Pacific Theological Seminary, 1995).
[23]Gailyn Van Rheenen, *Communicating Christ in Animistic Contexts* (Pasadena, CA: William Carey Library, 1991), 21.
[24]Keener, 2661-2.
[25]Kraft, *Christianity in Culture,* 113.
[26]Kraft, *Christian Witness,* 11-2.

West is to highlight the worldview assumptions that need transformation in the light of Scripture while at the same time honoring and building connections with the various cultures.

But that transformation is seldom total. Walls observes:

> Rarely, however, are worldviews entirely destroyed and replaced by completely different ones. What usually happens is that people modify their maps of reality, adding the new information correcting the ideas they now see as wrong, altering the relationship of one set of ideas to another, making some bigger, some smaller, crossing out some altogether.[27]

Several questions arise for consideration. How modified are the maps of the people in our churches in our culture and what is our role in addressing this issue? Second, what cultural assumptions serve as bridges to biblical theology? Third, what cultural assumptions should be modified or overturned by such a theology? Fourth, where have we assumed that our culture is a bridge when in fact it is at least partially a barrier to biblical truth and Christian maturity? The limitations of this essay suggest that answering these questions is beyond our scope here. This kind of inquiry is necessary in order to more effectively train Christian leaders who can impact their culture.

The Jews

In Pisidian Antioch, Paul affirms the Jews' monotheistic worldview and the authority of the OT, which provides a bridge between them and Paul's theology of the Messiah. Where he challenges that worldview is with the idea that the promised Messiah was none other than Jesus of Nazareth, who came not as the political revolutionary that the Jews expected, but as one who would bear the shame of the cross and be resurrected from the dead.

---

[27] Walls, 37.

The Athenians

Here, Paul also found common ground. He affirmed that God does exist, that he is sufficient in himself and that he does not dwell in the temples of men.[28] Paul affirmed the supernatural causality in their worldview and affirmed that things like the weather, crops, and human life, etc., were created and overseen by a power beyond the natural realm. Also, a number of the terms he uses such as "world" (17:24), "his offspring" (17:28) and, "the divine" (17:29), would have resonated well with the philosophers who were listening to him.[29] But as Flemming notes, this identification can only go so far.[30]

What he challenged was their polytheism by contending that these things were created and maintained by one God, not a multitude of gods, goddesses and other spirits. By starting with the God of creation, he undercuts and seeks to shrink their mental maps by contending that only in this God do we "live and move and have our being" (17:28).

The idea of the gods dying and being resurrected, often in connection with various seasons, was common in the mythology of ancient Greece.[31] The idea of the resurrection of Christ, however, including a call to repentance, righteous living and a warning about future judgment, at least in the sense of moral accountability, was well beyond their comprehension.[32] Here, Paul seeks to dramatically change their worldview by advocating a God who will hold them accountable for their lifestyles.

Transformation of worldview calls for affirming the biblical aspects of a people's worldview. Transformation also requires respectfully replacing that which is non-biblical with the truth of God's word, without compromising the truth in the process.

---

[28]Flemming, 79.
[29]Ibid., 78.
[30]Ibid., 79.
[31]https://utopianfrontiers.com/resurrection-mythology/ (accessed June 13, 2018).
[32]Keener is correct in noting that most Greeks expected future judgment for having angered the gods while still alive, but not in the sense of moral accountability by a moral and immutable deity (Keener, 2671).

How Culture Shapes Theology in Asia

Culture, especially worldview, shapes the way we do theology because we all read the Bible through our cultural lenses. Different cultures read the Bible differently because the prescription in our lenses is not the same. They also ask different questions of Scripture, questions shaped by their cultural environment.[33] In this sense also, then, doing theology is also a human construct.[34] As Kraft notes, "our theology must be informed by anthropology. . . ."[35]

Simon Chan adds that while culture must not be the source of theology, "cultural experiences may provide an important context for theology by posing questions that theology must address."[36] Theology must address real issues. When people come to Christ out of an animistic, or folk Islamic, Buddhist or Hindu background, they come with their mental maps already in place. As noted before, when they come to know Christ, the mental maps are redrawn but are not completely eradicated. How these maps are to be redrawn is a challenge for those of us who teach and do theology in Asia. What parts of their worldview can be affirmed? What must be challenged? What must be added or deleted? When people come to Christ, how should they recategorize their worldview? How should they understand their past traditions and religious practices?[37] For example, how should one understand the Holy Spirit as compared to the other spirits in the worldviews of Asia?[38] These must be among the tasks of the Asian theologian today. To do this well, one needs to understand

---

[33]The way we do theology is also shaped by the theological traditions in which we are raised or trained, but this is beyond the scope of this essay.

[34]Kraft, *Christianity and Culture*, 118.

[35]Ibid.

[36]Simon Chan, *Grassroots Asian Theology: Thinking the Faith from the Ground Up*, (Downer's Grove, IL: Inter-Varsity Press, 2014), 18.

[37]In a new book recently released by APTS Press, Korean scholar Sang Yun Lee provides a good example by looking at things like Korean shaman traditions without necessarily demonizing them. See Sang Yun Lee, *A Theology of Hope: Contextual Perspectives in Korean Pentecostalism* (Baguio City, Philippines: APTS Press, 2018).

[38]I have attempted to do this in the Philippine context. See Dave Johnson, "Baptism in the Holy Spirit vs. Spirit Possession in the Lowland Philippines: Some Considerations for Discipleship," in *A Theology of the Spirit in Doctrine and Demonstration: Essays in Honor of Wonsuk and Julie Ma*, ed. Teresa Chai, 205-226 (Baguio City, Philippines: APTS Press, 2014).

the questions that people are asking. To not do so runs the risk of becoming irrelevant to the people we serve. If Paul had preached to the Jews the same way he spoke to the Athenian philosophers, he would not have had the impact he did. Vice versa is also true. Paul adapted his presentation of the gospel message to the worldview of his audience without compromising the message or removing the offense of the cross.

Challenges to Impacting Culture in the Theological Classroom

The implications for theological education are enormous. The passages selected for this paper were chosen, in part, to illuminate the need for critical reflection on these issues in the Asian context.

The Separation of Theological and Anthropological Studies

One of the problems is that studies in cultural anthropology are often relegated to a seminary's missions department and are not integrated into the main theological curriculum. Animism, if taught at all, is an elective even in the missions department, although it may also be included as a section of a world religions course. For most Bible schools, cultural anthropology and animism are not even a part of the curriculum, at least in the schools of my denomination, the Assemblies of God.

Western Theological Curriculum

Part of the reason for this lack is that Asian schools at both the Bible college and seminary level have adopted their theological curriculum from the West. As Das notes, historically seminary curriculum has been a "fairly standard package that was transported across cultures and continents and was not sensitive to local culture, traditions and values."[39] Hwa Yung, writing about the need for an Asian systematic theology, states: "Asian Christians need a framework

---

[39] Rupen Das, *Connecting Curriculum with Context: A Handbook for Context Relevant Curriculum Development in Theological Education* (Carlisle, UK: London Global Library, 2015), 1.

within which to think about God's revelation of himself and his activity in the world, in the context of their own cultures and missiological tasks that they face."[40] This also applies to theological education.

Lack of Interdisciplinary Studies

Another factor is the lack of emphasis on being interdisciplinary. In a landmark essay at the founding of the Asia Theological Association (ATA) in 1974, Indian scholar Saphir Athyal called for interpreting the Bible through Asian eyes, which would call for an interdisciplinary approach that would include cultural anthropology and responses to other Asian religions.[41] According to Lee, not much progress has been made so far.[42]

Asian Scholars Trained in the West

A third factor is that many Asian scholars were trained in the West, which gave them little or no opportunity to reflect on Asian issues. Gener records his own experience:

> Most of us Asian biblical scholars and theologians were trained in Euro-American academies which denied us the opportunity to bring our Asian ecclesial issues, congregational experiences, and cultural concerns into our writing and theologizing. Our perpetuation of this disconnect between biblical and theological scholarship and contextual ecclesial experience has produced an academic environment that tends

---

[40]Hwa Yung, *Mangoes or Bananas?: The Quest for an Authentic Asian Christian Theology*, Regnum Studies in Mission, Oxford, UK: Regnum Books International, 228.

[41]Saphir F. Athyal, "Toward an Asian Christian Theology" in *What Asian Christians Are Thinking: A Theological Source Book*, 68-84 (Quezon City, Philippines: New Day Publishers, 1976), 78-79. Cf. also Timoteo D. Gener, "Doing Contextual Systematic Theology in Asia," *Journal of Asian Evangelical Theology*, vol. 22, 1-2 (March—September 2018), 55.

[42]Moonjang Lee, "Asian Theology," in *Global Dictionary of Theology: A Resource for the Worldwide Church,* ed. William Dyrness, Veli-Matti Karkkainen, Juan Francisco Martinez and Simon Chan. (Downer's Grove, IL: Inter-Varsity Press, 2006), 76. Cf. Gener, "Doing Contextual," 54.

to stifle the development of new theological insights which are crucial for the growth of Asian evangelical theology.[43]

The result has not been positive. Gener goes on to say, "When theologians are so detached from the church's daily life, it is not surprising that they have little of value to say to the church."[44]

Western Theological Literature

A fourth factor is that most of the literature in Asian theological libraries is from the West. Since western authors, like anyone else, write within their cultural context and so do not cover Asian issues. While there is certainly much to be gained from these writings, Asian students often do not have answers to the questions they bring to the classroom. For example, Tim Gener notes that Milliard Erickson's *Christian Theology* devotes only a few pages to issues like demon possession, poverty and injustice, all of which are dominant issues in Asia.[45]

Encouraging Trends

Thankfully, there are some encouraging trends. The first is the development of the Langham Partnership Scholarship program, started by the late John R. W. Stott in 1969 to improve theological training in the Majority World. Since then 266 scholars have received their terminal degrees, mostly PhDs, and have returned home to start and/or serve in Bible colleges and seminaries in their homelands, some launching their own PhD programs. In the beginning, all scholarship awardees went to the West to study. However, as a result of their labors in Majority World seminaries, some began studying in these programs and Langham now claims that 36% of the scholarship awardees are studying in the Majority World, something that would have been difficult to accomplish a generation ago.[46] Beginning in 2010,

---

[43]Gener, "Doing Contextual," 56.
[44]Ibid., 57.
[45]Ibid., 49-50, see Milliard J. Erickson, *Christian Theology*, 3rd ed. (Grand Rapids: Baker, 2013), 502-03, 597-599, 763-768.
[46]Ibid.

Langham began offering post-doctoral fellowships where participants could go to various schools in the West for research, writing and reflecting.[47] While there is no guarantee that these scholars will teach, write and reflect on issues in their home cultures, the Langham scholars that I personally know are doing so and are doing it well.

Second, there are a growing number of seminaries worldwide that now have programs in World Christianity. In an informal survey conducted by noted Asian theologian Wonsuk Ma, there are at least thirty seven seminaries in the West and elsewhere that have masters and/or doctoral programs in the study of Global Christianity, where theological, missiological, ecclesiastical and historical issues that are indigenous to the Majority World can be researched and reflected upon, often in a multi-cultural environment that encourages inter-disciplinary dialogue.[48] As many as eleven more schools are planning to add such a program within the next three years.[49]

A third encouraging trend is that more Majority World scholars are writing for publication. While some of these scholars choose to write on western theological themes, the majority appear to be writing within their own contexts and are addressing local or regional theological, missiological, and sociological issues. This bodes well for providing library resources and textbooks for theological institutions in Asia that deal with Asian cultural and theological issues, but the need is still much greater than the supply.

One challenge in this regard, however, is that a number of these works are being published through publishing houses and journals in the West, often at a price that most non-westerners cannot afford. Again, Langham and others are addressing this issue and there is hope on the horizon, but much more needs to be done.

---

[47]https://hk.langham.org/what-we-do/langham-scholars/our-history/ (accessed August 14-15, 2018).
[48]Wonsuk Ma, *Global Christianity Programs Survey*, March, 2018.
[49]Ma, *Global Christianity*.

A Call for a Research Culture

To facilitate these trends, research cultures need to be created on college and seminary campuses in the Majority World to provide authors with the time and atmosphere needed to reflect and write on the intersection of Asian theological and cultural issues to serve the needs of the Asian church.

Conclusion

The purpose of the paper was to demonstrate how cultural anthropology can enhance our understanding of how to do theology in Asia, using the biblical text as an example and drawing implications for theological education in Asia. In the first part, attention was given to defining and explaining how worldview impacts the way people see the world, particularly when it comes to religion. In the biblical references cited, Paul demonstrates how understanding the worldview of the hearer can impact and enhance the teaching of the truth and bring worldview transformation in order to help people come to know Christ in their context. Following Paul's example will help us answer not only the questions raised earlier, but the myriad of questions that are raised as we apply ourselves to the task of doing theology in Asia.

The second part focused on the situation of theological education, dealing with both the challenges and the encouraging trends set by those striving to address the issues articulated and meeting the needs of the Asian churches. This part also calls for much more work to be done.

References Cited

Arnold, Clinton E. *The Colossian Syncretism: The Interface Between Christianity and Folk Belief at Colossae.* Grand Rapids: Baker Book House, 1996.

_____. *Power and Magic: The Concept of Power in Ephesians.* Grand Rapids: Baker Book *House,* 1992.

_____. *Powers of Darkness: Principalities & Powers in Paul's Letters.* Downer's Grove, IL: Inter-Varsity Press, 1992.

Athyal, Saphir. "Toward an Asian Christian Theology." In *What Asian Christians Are Thinking: A Theological Source Book.* Quezon City, Philippines: New Day Publishers, 1976.

Chan, Simon. *Grassroots Asian Theology: Thinking the Faith from the Ground Up.* Downer's Grove, IL: Inter-Varsity Press, 2014.

Das, Rupen. *Connecting Curriculum with Context: A Handbook for Context Relevant Curriculum Development in Theological Education.* Carlisle, UK: Langham Global Library, 2015.

Erickson, Milliard J. *Christian Theology.* 3rd Edition. Grand Rapids: Baker, 2013.

Flemming, Dean. *Contextualization in the New Testament: Patterns for Theology and Mission.* Downer's Grove, IL: Inter-Varsity Press, 2005.

Gener, Timoteo. "Doing Contextual Systematic Theology in Asia: Challenges and Prospects." *Journal of Asian Evangelical Theology.* Vol. 22, Nos. 1-2. (March-September 2018), 49-68.

Hiebert, Paul G. *Anthropological Insights for Missionaries.* Grand Rapids: Baker Book House, 1985.

_____. *Cultural Anthropology.* 2nd Ed. Grand Rapids: Baker Book House, 1983.

Hurtado, Larry. *Destroyer of the Gods: Early Christian Distinctiveness in the Roman World.* Waco, TX: Baylor University Press, 2016.

Johnson, Dave. "Baptism in the Holy Spirit vs. Spirit Possession in the Lowland Philippines: Some Considerations for Discipleship." In *A Theology of the Spirit in Doctrine and Demonstration: Essays in Honor of Wonsuk and Julie Ma.* Ed. Teresa Chai, 205-226. Baguio City, Philippines: APTS Press, 2014.

Keener, Craig S. *Acts: An Exegetical Commentary.* Volume 3. Grand Rapids: Baker Academic, 2014.

Kraft, Charles H. *Anthropology for Christian Witness.* Maryknoll, NY: Orbis Books, 1996.

_____. *Christianity and Culture: A Study in Dynamic Biblical Theologizing in Cross-Cultural Perspective.* Maryknoll, NY: Orbis Books, 1979.

Lee Moonjang. "Asian Theology." In *Global Dictionary of Theology: A Resource for the Worldwide Church* Eds. William Dyrness,

Veli-Matti Karkkainen, Juan Francisco Martinez and Simon Chan. Downer's Grove, IL: Inter-Varsity Press, 2006.

Lee, Sang Yun. *A Theology of Hope: Contextual Perspectives in Korean Pentecostalism.* Baguio City, Philippines: APTS Press, 2018.

Parshall, Phil. *Bridges to Islam.* Grand Rapids: Baker Book House, 1983.

Richardson, Don. *Eternity in Their Hearts.* Rev. Ed. Ventura, CA: Regal Books, 1981.

Roxborogh, W. John. "Situating Southeast Asian Christian Movements in the History of World Christianity. In *Christian Movements in Southeast Asia: A Theological Exploration.* Ed. Michael Nai-Chiu Poon. 19-38. Singapore: Genesis Books, 2010.

Stott, John R.W. *The Spirit, The Church and The World: The Message of Acts.* Downer's Grove, IL: Inter-Varsity Press, 1990. https://utopianfrontiers.com/resurrection-mythology/ (accessed June 13, 2018).

Van Rheenen, Gailyn. *Communicating Christ in Animistic Contexts.* Pasadena, Ca: William Carey Library, 1991.

Walls, Andrew F. *Cross Cultural Frontiers: Studies in the History of World Christianity.*

Maryknoll, NY: Orbis Books, 2017.

INNOVATION IN CHRISTIAN HIGHER EDUCATION: The Case of the Oxford Centre for Mission Studies

Julie Ma

Introduction

It is my privilege to contribute an article to the volume honoring the McKinney's. Their long mission service in training and educating leaders in many countries has been exemplary. Their passion and dedication have influenced countless church and mission leaders in Asia and other continents.

Oxford Centre for Mission Studies (OCMS), Oxford UK, was founded in 1983 by global Evangelical leaders. The school's goal is to prepare global church and mission leaders in practice in, and research on, holistic mission. This "mission academic community" is made of mission practitioners.[1] OCMS is unique in several important ways, perhaps serving as an example for the future of Christian higher education which I have found and experienced when I taught there during the last 10 years (2006-2016).

OCMS is structured in such a way as to accommodate almost every imaginable mission and theological subject for research. This potential owes to the British higher education system and the innovative academic structure of OCMS. The institution also serves the churches in the Global South (or earlier designated as the "Two-Thirds World", a term replacing "Third World" and indicates

---

[1] Wonsuk Ma, "Holistic Mission, Theological Education and OCMS: An Editorial," *Transformation* 28: 4 (2011), 233-234.

approximately 2/3 of the world's population). In the inception of the school, the founders foresaw the rapid growth of Christianity in Africa, Asia, and Latin America. On the other hand, the churches in Europe and North America continued to decline in number and energy. The school took this radical change in the global Christian demography into consideration. The leaders sensed the huge implications of this change on defining mission, practice, and constructing a theology to undergird the continuing change. Walls explicates on global theological education:

> The Christian Church is now multicentric, its centers of energy widely dispersed across the world, so that major initiatives in mission – whether that mission be expressed in evangelism, social action, theological reflection or radical spirituality – may arise in any part of the world and be directed to any other part of it. This is a useful point with which to begin our thinking about global theological education, for churchly habits of mind, and the weight of tradition and the structures of theological institutions all tend to obscure the fact of that redrawing of the theological map. The redrawing has huge consequences, not only for theological education but for the theological scholarship which both informs theological education and is developed through it.[2]

At the same time, the large deposit of Christian knowledge, tradition, experiences, and resources are in the global North (or the West). The leaders contended that the preparation of future global leaders of the South would require the full resources of the West in the education process. The conclusion was to create a new academic structure in the heart of the western academic tradition but fully governed by the churches of the South. Thus came a revolutionary educational structure called the Oxford Centre for Mission Studies.

---

[2] Andrew Walls, "World Christianity, Theological Education and Scholarship," *Transformation* 28:4 (2011): 235.

According to my experiences from teaching at OCMS for ten years, students came from diverse countries to study various research subjects from their rich mission experiences. They produce remarkable research which makes a significant contribution to their churches and society and further global churches. Some even impacted international institutions on their policy-making process.

This study begins with a brief historical overview of the "emerging mission as Transformation" as part of the birth story of the school.[3] Then, it discusses theological education at OCMS in focus on transformational mission in connection with a holistic emphasis. The institution, at the same time, gives room to research traditional mission areas such as evangelism and church planting. This paper also deals with the impact of such educational enterprise by surveying selected graduates' contributions to their societies.

Historical Background

Major changes in politics, culture, and ethics took place in the world around the 1960s. "While some would describe the '60s as tumultuous, chaotic and even anarchic, others would depict that period as ushering in a new era of freedom and opportunity."[4] Liberation activism, predominantly among Roman Catholics in Latin America, started to rise up and powerfully stimulated the Church globally. The main concern was for the needy and the deprived as an essential mission work. However, not everyone who advocated the church's mandate towards the poor was motivated by liberation theology. Evangelical leaders of the Global South (a term replacing "Third World" indicating emerging countries, many of which are in the southern hemisphere) started practicing their "kingdom right" in constructing theology and mission theory. This movement soon led them to realize a unique obligation to make the Christian message and mission relevant to the socio-cultural contexts: a form of contextualization.[5]

---

[3]Al Tizon, "Mission as Education: a Past-to-Future Look at INFEMIT/OCMS," *Transformation,* 28:4 (2011), 255.
[4]Ibid., 254.
[5]Tizon, "Mission as Education, 254. See also, Chris Sugden, *Gospel, Culture and Transformation* (Oxford: Regnum Books International, 2000), 2-5.

In the Protestant sphere, the excitement of the 1960s formed the air for the rise of the dispute between ecumenical and evangelicals over the mission. In 1966, evangelicals held two historic conferences: in Wheaton, IL and Berlin. The year and the conferences marked the decisive division between the ecumenical and evangelical mission movements. Evangelicals by then felt that the ecumenical mission epitomized by the work of the World Council of Churches had miserably restrained the significance of evangelism.[6] And when ecumenicals met for the fourth gathering of the Council in Uppsala in 1968, the assembly produced what is called the Uppsala Report. Setting the priority of Christian mission as partaking "in the struggle for a just society," the Report drove a wedge in the growing gap between the two global mission movements.[7]

Evolving "Mission as Transformation"

In this chaotic situation, another type of mission theologian started to emerge, who became known later as "radical evangelicals."[8] Al Tizon helpfully characterized them:

These radical evangelical theologians and practitioners took seriously the revolutionary call upon the church to change society for the sake of the poor, but who refused to abandon evangelism as part of their interpretation of the historic, orthodox, Christian mission. They saw the gospel as demanding both evangelism and social concern in order, not only to be relevant in contexts of poverty, violence, and oppression but more fundamentally, to be faithful to the very nature of the gospel itself.[9]

---

[6]R. Hedlund, *Roots of the Great Debate in Mission* (Bangalore, India: Theological Book Trust, 1997), 156-163.
[7]Hedlund, *Roots of the Great Debate in Mission,* 223-232.
[8]Al Tizon, *Transformation after Lausanne: Radical Evangelical Mission in Glocal-Local Perspective* (Oxford, UK: Regnum books International, 2008), 3-4.
[9]Tizon, "Mission as Education," 254.

The meeting of the radical evangelicals took place in 1973 in Chicago. This North American initiative also included by design like-minded evangelical leaders from the Two-Thirds World. The conference called to commit itself to evangelism and social justice.[10] However, the most historic and significant meeting in the development of evangelical holistic mission was the First International Congress on World Evangelization held in Lausanne, Switzerland in 1974. Called by Bill Graham, the renowned American evangelist, the Congress produced "The Lausanne Covenant" initially drafted by the English Anglican, John Stott. This official statement has fifteen definitive affirmations in Christian mission, and one of them was social responsibility.[11] The Lausanne gathering was a clear continuation of Chicago's emphasis on "social justice."

In the Lausanne Congress, a group of "radical evangelicals" consistently campaigned for the insertion of "social obligation" in the Covenant. Leaders such as Samuel Escobar and Rene Padilla both from Latin America, who later became founding members of OCMS, contributed to a declaration on "Radical Discipleship." The group assisted the Lausanne Covenant and also pressed for a more combined comprehension of the fullness of the gospel.[12] To express their conviction, they formed an ad hoc group known as the "Radical Discipleship Group," and produced a report titled, *Theology Implications of Radical Discipleship*. The group offered it to the representatives both as a supplement and a remedial to the Covenant.[13] It encouraged for an even stronger engagement to "social justice" in the world, as it endeavored to incorporate works of sympathy and impartiality into the mission of the Church. At the end, "over a third of the members signed the declaration and it was contained within the rest of the authorized Congress documents [which] testified to the

---

[10]Ron J. Snider, "The Chicago Declaration," in *the Chicago Declaration*, ed. R.J. Snider (Carol Stream, IL: Creation House, 1974), 1-2. In this same volume, some of the original signers of the Declaration, including Samuel Escobar, Nancy Hardesty and Jim Wallis, offer their reflections.

[11]Tizon, "Mission as Education," 254.

[12]Sugden, "A History of the Oxford Center for Mission Studies," 266.

[13]J.D. Douglas "Theology Implications of Radical Discipleship," in *Let the Earth Hear His Voice,* ed. J.D. Douglas (Minneapolis, MN: World Wide Publications, 1975), 1294-1296.

impact of the radical element upon the evangelical missionary community."[14]

But, if the "radicals" at the Lausanne Congress anticipated a total agreement on the social responsibility of the Church as part of mission, they were proven completely wrong. The ensuing sharp disputes over this issue resulted in what is called the "decade after the Congress." The dispute climaxed at the Consultation on World Evangelization (COWE) in 1980 in Pattaya, Thailand, and the Consultation on the Relationship between Evangelism and Social Responsibility (CRESR) in 1982 in Grand Rapids, Michigan. In spite of some agreements in these meetings, fundamental disagreements surfaced on "evangelicalism concerning the place of social concern in the mission of the church."[15] It was in the 1983 meeting in Wheaton under the theme, "I Will Build My Church," that radical evangelicals were able to articulate their insistence of social responsibility in the word "transformation", so "Mission as Transformation" was the term agreed upon. Vinay Samuel and Chris Sugden provided the following summary in 1999: "Transformation is to enable God's vision of society to be actualized in all relationships, social, economic and spiritual so that God's will be reflected in human society and his love be experienced by all communities, especially the poor."[16]

Since the "holistic missionary movement took on the name Transformation," its exponents have gradually spread their conviction throughout the world. They challenged churches and missionaries not to fall into the trap of "evangelization without liberation, church planting without community building," the shift of mind without altering social buildings, and "vertical reconciliation between God and humanity without horizontal reconciliation between humanity and humanity."[17]

---

[14] Tizon, "Mission as Education," 254.
[15] Ibid., 255.
[16] Chris Sugden, "Transformational Development: Current State of Understanding and Practice," *Transformation* 20:2 (2011), 73.
[17] Tizon, "Mission as Education," 255.

Formation of OCMS

Theological Education and Transformative Mission

Ideal theological formation and education require building the foundation on scripture and theology, the use of cultural sensitivity, social relevancy and high quality education. The advocates of the "transformational movement" stressed the critical need to develop profound thinking in the work of mission in the world. This emphasis needs to be understood in the context of the growing focus of the Lausanne community on strategies. Many meetings were held to forge practical strategies to reach the lost. The "unreached peoples" concept is one good example. As a result, often "theology [took] a backseat to strategic initiatives."[18] The transformation mission leaders consistently argued that the sustenance and growth of the new mission concept necessitated a system to produce mission theologies and mission theologians. If this new concept of mission was birthed out of the realities of life and mission in the Two-Thirds World, they concluded, its leadership should undertake the task of the construction of the transformation (and holistic) mission.

At the Pattaya Conference (1980), the radical evangelical leaders shared a need for several academic components. First, an organizational center was necessary to continually advance the issues of the "holistic gospel." The center would facilitate scholars' research and its application in mission. The center would bring together scholars and mission practitioners to foster an ongoing learning process. Ideas would have come from mission practices in diverse contexts. The themes included "urban mission, development, and other faiths." They also discussed a need for publications to advance the concept of holistic mission. In June 1982, shortly after the Bangkok Consultation, the groundwork assembly occurred in Michigan which produced the document, "The Church in Response to Human Need." The conference was held in Wheaton in June 1983 where the expression "Mission as Transformation" was formally adopted.

---

[18]Vinay Samuel and Chris Sugden, eds. *Mission as Transformation: A Theology of the Whole Gospel* (Oxford England: Regnum Books International), xi, 1999.

Again, the participants re-affirmed their commitment to the establishment of an "institutional presence to draw together and inspire and promote this understanding."

Founding of OCMS

Going back to the Pattaya meeting, the idea of a study center for holistic mission was specifically explored. Sugden details the discussion:

> At the Pattaya Consultation, Rev Vinay Samuel from India came with a colleague from India, Rev Chris Sugden, a new missionary from England, and met Dr David Cook, an ethics lecturer at Oxford. With the other scholars, Dr Rene Padilla, Dr Kwame Bediako, Dr Orlando Costas, Dr Ron Sider and Bishop David Gitari, they envisioned a process by which scholars could come with research topics in the field of holistic mission, be enrolled in a research institution for a post-graduate degree, spend 6 weeks to 3 months a year there, and for the remainder of their year be involved in their normal mission calling in Africa or Asia. This process would root the scholar in their mission setting; it would derive study and research topics from the reality of that setting, it would avoid the need to relocate the scholar's family to the West and thus avoid the pressure on the scholar to relocate permanently. At the same time, it would provide accreditation that could command global respect in the global conversation.[19]

An important question was raised: where must the research institution be situated? They analyzed among themselves about the location and that America had quite many deep-rooted mission centers. Could a Two-Thirds World institution be established there? The answer was negative because the "accreditation process for

---

[19]Sugden, "A History of the Oxford Center for Mission Studies," 267. See also 'INFEMIT', http://www.infemit.net/. And also see 'INFEMIT News', *Transformation* 32:3 (Aug. 1991).

research degrees would not allow the development of the non-residential component." The United States' educational procedures paid attention to key structural and institutional requirements such as buildings, libraries, competent faculty, assessments, governance, and policies and regulation.[20]

Fortunately, David Cook recognized great potential in the English higher education system with its established stability and flexibility to accommodate the radical structure required to accomplish the educational vision. In the United Kingdom, the "Council of National Academic Awards" had set up a procedure to recognize research degrees in non-residential study modes. It provided liberty that was remarkably promising. Numerous scholars at Oxford had expressed a need to make considerable theological sources available to serve the rising global church. David Cook's suggestion to locate at Oxford was seriously considered. He was assisted by Chris Sugden who had a vast knowledge of the city and its educational resources.[21] Global mission leaders also supported this exploration. "Over 1982–1983 Dr. Orlando Costas personally encouraged and commissioned Rev. Vinay Samuel to take responsibility to make this venture happen. The founding fathers asked Chris Sugden to return with his family from India to Oxford to work with David Cook to establish the institution."[22]

OCMS was finally opened in 1983 by a group of transformation mission leaders who later organized themselves as the International Fellowship of Evangelical Mission Theologians (INFEMIT) in 1987. They included the late Orlando Costas, Vinay Samuel, Rene Padilla, Chris Sugden, Melba Maggay, Ron Sider, David Gitari, Kwame Bediako, Tito Paredes, and Tom Sine.[23] INFEMIT and OCMS operated under the same board of directors and leadership.[24] It was a stirring time in the evangelical mission world which was expressed in global mission conferences.

---

[20]Ibid., 267.
[21]Ibid., 268.
[22]Ibid.
[23]INFEMIT, "History" http://infemit.org/about/history/ (accessed July 18, 2018).
[24]Tizon, *Transformation after Lausanne: Radical Evangelical Mission in Global-Local Perspective*, 76.

The Oxford Centre for Mission Studies has endeavored to make its ideal into a reality.[25] By design, OCMS has offered graduate and post-graduate programs to prepare the leaders who would train leaders. From the beginning, the Two-Thirds World churches have been given the privileged place.[26] Also, they agreed that Christian mission practitioners should be encouraged to bring their frontline experience and data to the construction of mission theologies. But this was carried out within the British higher education system with its "western" tuition fees, and the school operated in one of the most expensive places in the West–Oxford!

OCMS leadership had to "think outside the box," since the western way of advanced education has not been traditionally approachable by people from the Two-Thirds World who desire to receive education in their institutes. The "unwelcome mat" for those from the Two-Thirds World is placed down in diverse ways.[27] Tizon elaborates,

> OCMS has tried hard to address these obstacles. By keeping costs down, developing a field-based, mentor-based program, and establishing partnerships with other academic institutions around the world, INFEMIT/OCMS has valiantly attempted to provide accredited theological education, primarily for leaders and scholars from the non-Western world, while keeping fresh, creative, holistic, and contextually relevant theology at the center of missiological reflection. OCMS' self-description says in part, "In its 25 years of ministry, we have brought . . . topics [such as poverty alleviation, social conflict, corruption, community development, the media, education, HIV/AIDS, etc.] into mission thinking with academic

---

[25]Tizon, "Mission as Education," 253.
[26]Ibid., 256.
[27]Ibid., 257. The "unwelcome mat" is demonstrated in various ways: the huge cost of graduate education; "the institutional structures and procedures which is the Western bureaucratic machinery as well as Westernized instruction, exams and grades given by Western faculty; has to do with content . . . students have had to go through Augustine, Luther, Calvin, Aquinas, Wesley, Barth. . ."

credibility and spiritual sensitivity, through post-graduate and post-doctoral research.[28]

University Affiliations

The dream of OCMS is to offer a world-class education for the leaders of the Global South within the British university system. An element of this operation is the validation of a chartered university. An independent college or center does not have a degree-granting power—only a university does.

The earliest validation was started by Stewart Weir, the administrator of the Council of National Academic Awards (CNAA), in 1986. He came to the Centre and evaluated the quality of the academic program and resources of OCMS. In the meantime, the CNAA was incorporated into the Open University. OCMS leaders contended that the British system of certifying courses and programs was most appropriate for OCMS.[29] The school could construct its own programs to best accomplish its vision and mission, and the validating institution would assess the quality of education.

Later, OCMS offered programs validated by the University of Wales around the 1990s. At the initial five-year assessment, the University of Wales invited OCMS to receive official recognition as an affiliated institution. It was understood that such recognition was usual for an institution with only a five-year partnership.[30]

Leeds University also became another partner around the 1990s, validating OCMS's first MA courses. They were also validated later by Wales University. MA courses in Development and HIV/AIDS were offered in countries where HIV/AIDS were prevalent: Kenya, Indonesia, India some other countries.[31] Professor Haddon Wilmer suggested that it might be beneficial for numerous MA students to register for the PhD with the University of Leeds because, with an enthusiastic Theology Department, they could afford supervision,

---

[28]Tizon, "Mission as Education," 28:4 (2011), 257.
[29]Sugden, "A History of the Oxford Center for Mission Studies," 271.
[30]Ibid., 272.
[31]Bernard C Farr, "Retrospective: Reflections on the OCMS International Programmes Project (1997-2007)," *Transformation* 28:4 (2011), 284.

particularly in African research.³² The MA programs came to an end as the institution moved its focus to the post-graduate programs, that is, Master of Philosophy (MPhil) and Doctor of Philosophy (PhD).

After the disintegration of the University of Wales due to its proliferation of validations overseas, OCMS, like many small colleges, quickly forged a new relationship with Middlesex University in 2012. This relationship continues to date.

The University of Oxford was on the list of potential partner universities nearly from the beginning of OCMS. In fact, an arrangement was made in 1985 to allow the candidates to enter the Oxford University Certificate in Theology program, with a specialty in Development Studies and Communication Studies. Applicants were registered with Wycliffe Hall, attended their lectures, and took the exams from the university. The residence was obligatory for around six months a year over two years. Students from the Philippines, New Zealand, and Mexico were experiencing success. However, a few years later, the relationship with Oxford University discontinued.³³ Part of the challenges may have been the residency requirement and the high tuition rates of the university.

Innovations in Mission Higher Education

The innovation and uniqueness of the structure, contents, delivery, and outcome of the post-graduate education at OCMS has been distinctive. They are to fulfill the unique vision of the institution and its stakeholders. Some of them are as follows.

Student Demography

A global institution such as OCMS will have to negotiate diverse educational systems. To begin with, most students at OCMS are admitted as "non-traditional students," in the standards of British higher education. That is, most students do not usually come with a graduate research qualification (normally a master's degree). For

---

³²Sugden, "A History of the Oxford Center for Mission Studies," 273.
³³Ibid.

example, a Master of Divinity, extremely common in ministerial education, is not considered a valid preparation for a research postgraduate degree, unless it contains a serious thesis and supporting courses.

Secondly, many students come from different disciplines: economics, development studies, ethics, health, education, politics, and many more. Theology is only part of this wide spectrum of disciplines. Thirdly, related to the above, most of the students are not teaching or doing research in institutional settings: they are practitioners. Their professional work varies widely, but with one commonality: everyone uses their profession as God's gift to them, and not their gift to God's mission. The diversity of their work is brought together into one platform: mission.

Fourthly, most are mid-career adult learners. A survey of one cohort (about a dozen students) revealed that the average age of the students was forty-two, with eighteen years of mission practice. Given the demanding circumstances they are working in, normal academic life including reading and writing had not been part of their daily work. On the other hand, they bring extremely valuable data for their cutting-edge research: experience and field data. They are extremely motivated.

Fifthly, as intended, most students have been part-timers in their studies. The recent tight visa regulations of the British government motivated the school to resort to the part-time study mode. However, there were several full-time students with their families. Between 2006 and 2016, among the graduates, only two failed to return to their home country or country of work. Both were full-time students. And the administration concluded that the time the full-time students took to complete their studies was not necessarily shorter than the part-time students. As argued above, the founding leaders recognized the value of uninterrupted mission engagement to make the studies relevant and valuable, while the studies also contribute to the improvement of their mission practices. In spite of these important values of part-time study, typical British universities were unable to accept students for part-time studies. Only recently, more universities are operating "external" studies for part-time students.

OCMS Induction Procedure

There are three areas to look at in process: firstly, it is the applicant's capability and assurance; secondly, it is the viability of the subject, and thirdly, it is the accessibility of sources such as "sources of information and tools of research." After evaluating the applicants' research capability and the commitment of its constituencies to their study, OCMS requires each student to go through a four-week induction school. This was originally designed as a research seminar, serving new research students from OCMS and other schools. Many fondly remember that John Stott faithfully spoke in each seminar for many years. This then evolved into a highly structured induction school. At one point (in the middle of the 2000s), the induction program lasted for ten weeks. The program takes the initial research concept and turns it into a fully developed research proposal. Arguably, diverse research methodologies form the important components of the process.

The induction school forms a cohort. During the weeks of lectures, discussions, and sharing of their research ideas, a strong bond is established among the group. Some relationships continue until the completion of the studies. Considering that most participants are practitioners, their mission perspectives and approaches are greatly enhanced due to their lively exchange of experiences. Many mission partnerships are formed out of this strong bond.

The induction school also serves as a leveling and matriculating process. Because of the different educational systems and varying levels of educational qualities, some applicants are admitted with conditions. The induction school provides an excellent opportunity to determine one's academic capabilities. Indeed, at the end of the induction period, every participant is evaluated as to whether they are allowed to begin the long research journey towards a post-graduate degree.

Global Supervisors

One genius of OCMS is its ability to accommodate almost every possible research subject in mission. From the beginning, the school has been conscious of the growing topics of mission studies, especially in holistic mission. A large amount of research was related to the issue of poverty, including cultural and religious values, women and children, corruption, civil wars, health issues such as sanitation and HIV/AIDS, education, microfinance, and others. Theological studies are also strong, as many mission cases form the construction of new mission theologies. The list of the dissertations, numbering more than 100, reveals this diversity.[34] An external academic study categorized OCMS dissertations as: a) traditional academic, e.g., evangelism and church planting: b) church and mission organization and leadership training (the research is concentrating on a common problem and does not pay much attention to its application in a particular context) and: c) various mission issues such as development, human trafficking, poverty and HIV/AIDS in different continents including Africa, Asia, America and Europe.[35]

Although it has a relatively small faculty (less than a dozen in the full-time equivalency), the school maintains more than 160 supervisors, most of whom are external to OCMS. Each student has at least two supervisors or sometimes three. A faculty member serves as a house tutor, who can help students' research work and assist them constructing a research proposal. Further, the faculty tutor helps to find the right supervisors. The representative of the validating university observed this unusual solution to supervision of the wide-range of topics:

> The choice of supervisors and the process of supervision are distinctive and interesting. OCMS has access not only to some 14 internal supervisors but over a hundred external supervisors drawn from Universities and theological institutions not only in the UK but from around the world. The list of potential supervisors is massively impressive, and each student is allocated [up] to two supervisors. In addition, once registered with the university, they also have an OCMS-

---

[34]OCMS, "Dissertation Abstracts," https://secure.ocms.ac.uk/abstracts/index.php?mid=443 (accessed July 20, 2018).
[35]D. P. Davies, "The Research Contribution of OCMS," *Transformation*, 28: 4 (2011), 280.

based house tutor to whom they can turn for basic advice in the first instance. The hazards of having two supervisors, as is now a requirement in most UK universities, are obvious.[36]

Educational Management

The inherent challenges for OCMS has been finding ways to keep the researchers in their mission setting, build academic capabilities, provide timely yet remote guidance, make resources available on site, and help them to produce credible dissertations. All of these may be achievable if the institution has all the necessary human, institutional, technological, and financial resources. The truth is that the school truly represented the Christian reality of the Global South: rich in zeal and growth, but poor in resources. This was where the mission hospitality of the West became crucial.

"Our goal [at OCMS] is to nurture relevant and engaged research for leaders at the cutting edge of Christian ministry and mission globally." It implies that students are in the mainstream of ministry by which they can produce significant research and make a contribution. This also symbolizes OCMS from the standard of the "research activity of departments of theology in the UK."[37]

Outcome of the OCMS Program

Research and Researchers

Over the years, the stream of students and visiting researchers has increased gradually. Around the turn of the century, the school had about 80 students which grew to nearly 100 by 2004. Currently, the number is around 120. With this number (all pursuing the post-graduate degrees, that is, Master of Philosophy or Doctor of Philosophy), the school is approximately comparable in size to the research school of a medium-sized university department.[38] It took

---

[36]Davies, "The Research Contribution of OCMS," 281.
[37]Ibid., 280.
[38]Informed by Wonsuk Ma who served as the Executive Director of OCMS from 2006-2016.

quite some time before any serious dissertations or theses were produced. The earliest graduate (MPhil) came out in 1989 and another in 1990.:

The first PhD was in 1991, and another MPhil followed in 1992; there were no graduates in 1993 and 1994, so it was a very slow start. Numbers increased a little thereafter with three graduates (two PhD and one MPhil) in 1995 and another three, including the first University of Wales graduate (a PhD) in 1996. 1997 was, by comparison, a bumper year with seven graduates (all PhD except one); four more graduated in 1998 and another two in 1999. 2000 was another bumper year with eight graduating, including one Leiden PhD. The period 2001–2005 was fairly quiet with, on average, three to four graduates per annum. From that point on the numbers graduating per annum have increased significantly, with an average of almost eight graduates each year between 2006 and 2010–there were ten in 2010, the largest number in any one year.[39]

Throughout its short history, 135 candidates received postgraduate degrees through two validating universities. Eighty-six (73 PhD and 13 MPhil) completed degrees through the Open University in the 22 years since 1989. Forty-nine (45 PhD and 4 MPhil) graduated through the University of Wales.[40] A growing number have completed their studies in recent years through Middlesex University.

Influence of the Graduates: Case Studies

The research is varied and powerful. To illustrate the kinds of mission research undertaken by OCMS scholars and their impact, I would introduce the work and study of two graduates: Joshua Banda (Zambia) and Philip Ouedraogo (Burkina Faso).

Joshua Banda is a Zambian Pentecostal bishop who pastors a large church in Lusaka. Through a series of encounters, he came to realize the extent and seriousness of the HIV/AIDS pandemic in his country. Contrary to his hope and assumptions, and to his horror, he learned that the presence of this devastating disease was as real inside the

---

[39]Davies, "The Research Contribution of OCMS, 284.
[40]Ibid.

church as outside it. He established the Circle of Hope (COH) in 2005 to offer a church-based prevention and holistic care for HIV/AIDS patients (including "free anti-retroviral treatment"), and their family members.[41] Openness to the AIDS test was the first step, but the formidable first hurdle for any program for HIV/AIDS prevention and care. However, the Circle of Hope began to earn the confidence of men, both within and without the church, and the test rate soon surpassed that of large government-operated centers. The Circle of Hope also approached the issue as a holistic matter. They dealt with the HIV/AIDS as medical, social, economic, educational, and spiritual issues. The outcome was astonishing:

> To date, COH has counseled and tested over 7,429 people, of whom 5,326 are HIV + and have been enrolled in care. Of the number that is positive, 2,310 are currently on full ART, of which 516 are children. A group more than 200 community adherence personnel, caregivers, and counselors, have sensitized, educated and monitored clients on treatment in their homes. Approximately 80 people visit the COH Centre per day, while 120 patients are enrolled monthly.[42]

The church-based HIV/AIDS care programs formed the Health Care Association of Zambia. Banda's Northmead Assembly's programs belong to it and play a leading role. The ministry of the Association has borne a large portion of the national HIV/AIDS prevention and care program. The Association operates over 50% of healthcare facilities in Zambia.[43] Christian involvement in this fight against this destructive force has significantly reduced the infection rate. As a consequence, Banda was requested to lead the National AIDS Council in 2007.[44]

---

[41] Joshua Banda, "Engaging with the Community, the Fight against AIDS," in *Good News from Africa: Community Transformation through the Church*, ed. Brian Woolnough (Oxford: Regnum Book International, 2013), 48.
[42] Ibid., 49.
[43] Ibid., 42.
[44] Wonsuk Ma, "A Pentecostal Reflection on Christian Unity in the New Christian Millennium" (a Paper Presented at Global Forum for the Future of World Christianity,

The "Lazarus Project" is one more social ministry of the church among AIDS orphans. The pandemic grew beyond the ability of the traditional extended family system, which had absorbed the responsibility to care for the orphans of AIDS-infected parents. The Project secured a 40-acre farm to house, educate, and guide the orphans who were often brought from the streets of Lusaka. The Project offers Christian holistic care in a community setting.[45] As it grew, about 70 children came to live with volunteer teachers and mentors. Both COH and the Lazarus Project have provided a wide range of care and help to the most vulnerable in society. Through all these programs, the power of the gospel become lived out and enacted. Banda, his church members, and numerous ministries, are all stimulated and inspired by the gospel command. They also frequently preach the gospel to HIV/AIDS patients, their families and children under their care. The declaration of the good news, and meeting the immediate necessities of the defenseless, have been part of the Project from the start.[46]

Philippe Ouedraogo is another African Pentecostal minister. The rate of girl's education in Burkina Faso was the lowest among the Francophone West African countries, which have recorded the world's lowest education rate all together.[47] Within the country, the northern states where Muslim concentration is denser records lower female education rates than the rest of the country. This situation is often attributed to the socio-cultural and religious bias in favor of education and resource allocation for boys. Consequently, girls have only a slim chance to even begin the very basic education. This has large social implications. "Female involvement in areas of child care, nutrition, physical work, freedom of movement and marriage" is severely restricted.[48] Women often marry at a young age, rear their younger siblings, become the agricultural workforce, and migrate to cities to be manual workers.

Jeju, Korea, May, 2015), 2. See also "A Changing Africa" Joshua Banda 1/1 https://www.youtube.com/watch?v=p3cB63qmoew, 2012.

[45]Banda, "Engaging with the Community," 44.

[46]Joshua Banda, "A Request," (an email message to the author, Sept. 9, 2015).

[47]Philippe Ouedraogo, *Female Education and Mission: A Burkina Faso Experience* (Oxford: Regnum Book International, 2004), 2.

[48]C. Brock and N. K. Cammish, *Factor Affecting Female Participation in Education in Seven Developing Countries*, 2nd ed. (London: DFID, 1997), 21.

Sensing this gloomy situation, in 1991 Philippe Ouedraogo led to form a network of churches and mission organizations to provide a second educational chance to girls: "In the same year, Association Evangélique d'Appui au Développement (AEAD) under his leadership signed an agreement with the National Institute of Literacy. This initiative was a response to the low literacy rate of the nation, as AEAD was seeking to bring its contribution to the national need for female education."[49]

In 1992, various churches, mission organizations, and Christian non-governmental organizations (NGOs) met together under AEAD to forge a plan for education. They agreed that this would be a Christian response to the national schooling requirements. The gathering brought together diverse Christian bodies to share their knowledge and means for the corporative work. A practicable educational plan was its focal point.[50] They agreed that local churches be fully utilized for its class activities.

Subsequently, from 2006, an "intense and accelerated nine-month educational program [called "Speed School"] has been set up in the northern region of the nation, where about 80% of its population is Islamic." By 2012, a total of 2,255 males and females between 9 and 12 years old, who never had a chance for primary education, had finished this program. After the nine-month accelerated program, 90% of them accomplished the equivalence of the third-year official primary education. They were then incorporated into the public school system of the country.[51] In addition, many local churches also run formal schools under AEAD. An overwhelming majority of the 5,035 students in this school system in 2008-2009 were girls (or 62.5%)."[52]

Churches quickly recognized education as a wonderful tool for winning children to Christ. From the period of 2012 and 2015, there were about 342 converts to Christ from the Speed School.[53] In other

---

[49]P. Ouedraogo, "A Request" (an email message to the author, Sept.1, 2015).
[50]Ma, "A Pentecostal Reflection on Christian Unity," 1.
[51]Ibid.
[52]Ibid.
[53]Philippe Ouedraogo, "Transforming Community through Education," in *Good News from Africa: Community Transformation through the Church*, ed., Brian Woolnough (Oxford, England: Regnum Books International 2013), 87. It explains that

schools, like the Protestant College in Ouagadougou, over 700 students came to Christ within the academic year 2014-15. AEAD presently operates eleven schools, where more than 5,000 children and adults receive their education while hearing the good news of Jesus Christ.[54]

Publications

From the early discussions on the academic structures for studies of holistic mission, OCMS has occupied the center of the knowledge-production scheme. At the same time, the dissemination of valuable knowledge was also part of the strategic plan. The stakeholders of INFEMIT/OCMS wanted to provide means through which to disperse the "transformational perspectives with the international missionary community." The journal *Transformation* was launched in 1984. The journal has appeared four times a year to foster a global conversation on mission and ethics. In 1987, through Regnum Books, a publishing program was established with three operations: in Oxford, Ghana (Regnum Africa) and California (Regnum USA). In earlier years, conference papers were published. The oldest series is *Regnum Studies in Mission*. From the second half of the 2000s, *Global Christianity Series* has been added, and then *Regnum Edinburgh Centenary Series* in 2009. *The Edinburgh Series* completed its historic 35-volume global and ecumenical mission series. It also added a new series to serve non-academic mission workers. Regnum has published books of holistic mission topics, often by non-western authors. Regnum titles are frequently selected among "Missiology Books of the Year" listed by the *International Bulletin of Mission Research*. Regnum Books states its mission as making available "quality from the Two-Third World, to ensure academic excellence and integrity from both younger and senior scholars and to provide balanced regional representation."[55]

Speed School is "aimed at those youngsters, aged 9-12, who have missed out on primary education and are thus not able to enter the national formal education schooling."
  [54]Ouedraogo, "A Request" states that this information on the Protestant College of Ouagadougou was reported on 26 August 2015 in the Assemblies of God Executive meeting by the principal Emmanuel Kalkoundo.
  [55]Tizon, *Transformation after Lausanne*, 78-79.

Conclusion

OCMS has been the academic center for the promotion and exploration of holistic and transformational mission. OCMS sees transformation as the central value and goal of mission. Vinay Samuel and Chris Sugden, the pioneers of the school, defined transformation: "Transformation is to enable God's vision of society to be actualized in all relationships, social, economic and spiritual, so that God's will be reflected in human society and his love be experienced by all communities, especially the poor."[56] Their vision of "mission as transformation," or holistic mission, has been fully studied through the post-graduate and publishing programs of OCMS/Regnum. The contribution of this global community has been felt in many sectors, ranging from academic institutions, mission networks, and international institutions.

One mission leader commented that OCMS was "lifted far beyond its weight," in its 35 years of ministry. Its innovations were truly ahead of its time. At one point, its PhD completion rate was greater than the UK higher education benchmark. Part of its success story has to do with the emergence of Christianity and its mission awareness in the Global South. Unlike the 1980s, "privileging the South" is no longer a concept to fight for. The same is true of the notion of holistic mission or "mission as transformation." The Lausanne meeting in Cape Town (2010) took the concept of holistic mission as a given. Thus, OCMS and its stakeholders may deserve commendations.

John Stott who was a prominent theologian, pastor, and one of the most influential scholars in the 20th century was involved in OCMS from its beginning. He said in his letter to OCMS:

> The Oxford Centre for Mission Studies (OCMS) is an organization with which I have been involved since its inception in 1983, and I have watched its development with great satisfaction. It is the conviction of OCMS, which I share that during this century many of the Influential leaders in the

---

[56] Chris Sugden, "Transformational Development: Current State of Understand and Practice," *Transformation*, 20: 2 (2003), 71.

church will come from the global south. My prayer is that the Gospel of Jesus Christ, which it has been my privilege to share with others in 65 years of ministry, may continue in the leadership and witness of a new generation, and that the work of OCMS through its postgraduate and research programmes will be a key part in this process.[57]

However, the future of this innovative school is equally challenging. The part-time, practice-based quality research programs increase. A number of regional theological institutions began to offer quality theological education at a fraction of the western education cost. Equally challenging is how one can convince the world that the institution is by, of, and for the Global South, while it still depends on western financial resources. From another angle, five challenges were listed by Al Tizon in order for the transformational mission movement to continue its cutting-edge leadership: "1) holistic mission with a renewed emphasis upon creation care, 2) mission *from* Christianity's new center, 3) the development of a *glocal* [global plus local] theology, 4) the development of an intercontextual theology, and 5) the ongoing formation of non-traditional theological education."[58] For the sake of the global church and its mission, more learning communities sharing the vision of OCMS should rise. The role of OCMS, therefore, is not yet done. It should endeavor to keep theology and mission integral, continue its creative thinking, and maintain its innovative operation to provide a leading service to God's church and its mission.

References Cited

Banda, Joshua. "Engaging with the Community, the Fight against AIDS." In *Good News from Africa: Community Transformation through the Church*. Edited by Brian Woolnough. Oxford: Regnum Book International, 2013.

_____. "A Changing Africa." 1/1 https://www.youtube.com/watch?v=p3cB63qmoew, 2012.

---

[57] John Stott, Personal Letter to OCMS, Sept. 2009.
[58] Tizon, "Mission as Education," 28: 4 (2011), 262.

Brock, C. and N. K. Cammish. *Factor Affecting Female Participation in Education in Seven Developing Countries.* 2nd ed. London: DFID, 1997.

Davies, D. P. "The Research Contribution of OCMS." *Transformation* 28:4 (Oct. 2011): 265-278.

Farr, Bernard C. "Retrospective: Reflections on the OCMS International Programmes Project (1997-2007)." *Transformation* 28:4 (Oct. 2011): 286-299.

Hedlund, R. *Roots of the Great Debate in Mission.* Bangalore, India: Theological Book Trust, 1997.

"INFEMIT." http://www.infemit.net/.

"INFEMIT News." *Transformation* 32:3 (Aug. 1991).

Ma, Wonsuk. "Pentecostal Gift to Christian Unity: Its Possibility in the New Global Context." *International Review of Mission* 107:1 (June 2018): 33-48.

———. "Holistic Mission, Theological Education and OCMS: An Editorial." *Transformation* 28: 4 (Oct. 2011): 233-234.

Ouedraogo, Philippe. "Transforming Community through Education." In *Good News from Africa: Community Transformation through the Church.* Edited by Brian Woolnough. Oxford, England: Regnum Book International, 2013.

———. *Female Education and Mission: A Burkina Faso Experience.* Oxford: Regnum Book International, 2004.

Snider, J. R. "The Chicago Declaration." In *the Chicago Declaration,* edited by J. R. Snider, 1-3. Carol Stream, IL: Creation House, 1974.

Douglas, J. D. "Theology Implications of Radical Discipleship." In *Let the Earth Hear His Voice,* edited by J. D. Douglas, 1294-1296. Minneapolis, MN: World Wide Publications, 1975.

———. "The Lausanne Covenant." In *Let the Earth Hear His Voice*, edited by J. D. Douglas, 3-9. Minneapolis, MN: World Wide Publications, 1975.

Samuel, Vinay and Chris Sugden, eds. *Mission as Transformation.* Oxford, England: Regnum Book International, 1999.

Sugden, Chris. "A History of the Oxford Center for Mission Studies." *Transformation* 28:4 (Oct. 2011): 265-278.

_____. "Transformational Development: Current State of Understanding and Practice." *Transformation* 20:2 (Oct. 2011): 70-82.

_____. *Gospel, Culture and Transformation*. Oxford, UK: Regnum Books International, 2000.

_____. *Radical Discipleship*. London: Hunt Barnard Printing, 1981.

Stott, John. Personal Letter to OCMS, Sept. 2009.

Tizon, Al. *Transformation after Lausanne: Radical Evangelical Mission in Global-Local Perspective*. Oxford UK: Regnum Books International, 2008.

_____. "Mission as Education: a Past-to-Future Look at INFEMIT/OCMS." *Transformation* 28: 4 (Oct. 2011): 253-264.

Walls, Andrew. "World Christianity, Theological Education and Scholarship." *Transformation* 28:4 (Oct. 2011): 235-240.

COLLABORATIVE PARTNERSHIPS IN APTS

Yee Tham Wan

Introduction

In 2004, I began to serve as a faculty member at the Asia Pacific Theological Seminary (APTS) in Baguio, Philippines. Since 2009, I have been privileged to serve as the President of APTS. My wife and I are fully supported by Malaysian churches and individuals through the Malaysian Assemblies of God World Missions Department (WMD). APTS is an international seminary pioneered by US Assemblies of God missionaries in 1964 to serve the Asia Pacific region. In 1988, the American missionaries took the initiative to draw national Assemblies of God leaders of the region into the leadership of the seminary. Since 1989, the seminary has been governed by an International Board with a majority of non-Americans.[1]

While primarily serving the Asia Pacific and Northern Asia regions,[2] students at APTS come from about twenty to twenty-five

---

[1] William Menzies and John Carter describe this International Board of APTS as "a clear illustration of the principal of collegiality and partnership that has been at the heart of the philosophy of the American Assemblies of God foreign missions vision." William W. Menzies and John F. Carter, *Reflections on Developing Asian Pentecostal Leaders: Essays in Honor of Harold Kohl*, ed. A. Kay Fountain (Baguio, Philippines: APTS Press, 2004), 108.

[2] This "Asia Pacific region" description perhaps needs to be explained. Originally, APTS was set up to serve the "East Asia and Pacific" countries – falling within the ambit of the Asia Pacific region of the AGWM. But, the APTS constituency was subsequently enlarged and the make-up of the APTS Board suggests that it now serves two regions within the AGWM. Article VIII, Section 1 of the APTS Constitution reads, "The Board of Directors of APTS shall consist of one representative from each of the General

different countries, including many from outside of these two regions. The full-time resident faculty currently come from the USA, Korea, Philippines, Japan, Taiwan and Malaysia. Part-time and adjunct faculty come from all over the world too, teaching on the main APTS campus in Baguio, Philippines and in APTS extension centers around the Asia Pacific region. All faculty are missionaries who do not receive remuneration of any sort from APTS. In fact, resident faculty must rent their homes on the campus. This international assembly of missionaries at APTS is a joy to work with.

I am the first person from outside of the American AG World Missions Department (AGWM) to serve as the President of APTS. One of my main tasks is to travel the Asia Pacific region to connect with national churches (especially Assemblies of God) and their leaders. Working within the international APTS community and traveling the region has contributed to my understanding about missions partnerships in the region. From this background, I offer my brief comments about such partnerships.

Paradigms of Missions Partnership

Financier-Partner

I quickly realized in my missionary experience that there is a lot of baggage with the word "partnership" in the missions context. People often assume that financing (or at least the major portion) should come from the partner who is perceived to be the more prosperous. This would often be assumed to be the partner from the West. I once talked with an American missionary about the possibility of partnering with a local national leader on a certain project. His curt reply was, "I am afraid of partnerships. All they want is money from us."[3] Even at APTS, with an Asian seminary president and the majority of stakeholders from non-Western countries, "partnership" is still commonly viewed as a euphemism for financial support. Changing this impoverished understanding of missions partnership is necessary before genuine partnership can be achieved. That is not easily

---

Councils of the Assemblies of God in the Asia Pacific and Northern Asia regions plus the AGWM Assemblies of God-USA and missionary representatives."

[3]From a casual conversation; identity withheld of person in question.

accomplished even with the increasing prosperity of the various economies in the region.

This "Financier-Partner" paradigm has been in place for so long that it has created a culture of dependency, which my colleagues from the West have often complained about. Actually, there is also a kind of backlash from this whole "Financier-Partner" idea. With the West (in the case of APTS, it is the American Assemblies of God) having invested so much over the years as the more prosperous partner, it is understandably very difficult to simply release the mission to the nationals. The hoped-for long term returns in institutional missions are often a continuing legacy that carry on the vision of the pioneers. However, local national partners who are able themselves to finance the work they have inherited may feel ownership and thus the right to modify or change the original vision of the pioneers. We have unwittingly built up a direct connection between money and ownership in missions when in fact we are all stewards. This direct connection between money and ownership in missions could be even more harmful to genuine partnerships than the culture of dependency.

Facilitator-Partner

Apart from the Financier-Partner, there is also the "Facilitator-Partner" in missions partnerships. The Facilitator-Partner idea may kick in when the financier-partner has decided that it has become unnecessary or even unhealthy to pour in any more money into their missions. However, with a longer history and greater exposure in missions, the original financier-partner may want to continue to help the new self-supporting mission. Sometimes, the motivation to help could be a desire to ensure that the original vision would be maintained. There is actually a lot of good that can be said about the Facilitator-Partner idea, especially as a transition to a more ideal partnership arrangement. It is irresponsible for the original Financier-Partner to suddenly drop everything and leave the field as if the Financier-Partner arrangement is the only viable partnership arrangement in missions. One seminary in the Philippines suffered when Western missionaries decided that their job was finished and left suddenly. This sudden and complete disengagement resulted in the seminary going into immediate decline.[4]

Collaborator-Partner

There is seldom a completely equal partnership in missions. This is perhaps inevitable considering that the original construct is that the missionary has come with something to give while the target missions needs what the missionary has to give. Both the Financier-Partner and Facilitator-Partner paradigms are necessarily unequal partnerships. The "Collaborator-Partner" concept,[5] where both parties in this partnership are viewed as equals, is theoretically the ideal model in our search for a genuine partnership. In a genuine collaboration, the partners work with the premise that both have something to give that the other party needs. There is thus a genuine need and respect for each other.

This kind of collaborative partnership does not have to wait until the missions church becomes "mature." At every point of its growth and development, the local leadership of the missions church will have something to offer. Even at the early stages of the relationship between the missionary and the local leadership, the local leadership provides the contacts and channels so that the missionary can reach the target groups. The missionary's understanding of the local culture and language will probably be dependent on the local leadership. Without the collaborative input of the locals, the missionary's work is made much more difficult.

Missions Partnerships in the Asia Pacific Region

There is of course a lot of overlap in these three models of partnerships and they almost never operate independently of each

---

[4]Name of seminary withheld.
[5]John Carter uses the term "Co-Active" to describe something similar. I prefer to use the term "Collaboration" so that emphasis is given to the idea of a synergistic partnership and each has an input in the other. John F. Carter, "The Indigenous Principle Revisited: Towards a Coactive Model of Missionary Ministry," *Asian Journal for Pentecostal Studies* 1:1, (January, 1998). http://www.apts.edu/aeimages//File/AJPS_PDF/98-1-carter.pdf.

other. Missions partnerships typically mix these three models, with various models being prominent at different times during the partnerships. In the Asia Pacific region, where the "maturity" of nations varies, these three models operate at different levels in different places. It is difficult to generalize because the situation in this region is so diverse.[6] I need to be discreet when naming and describing some countries and avoid making general comments that could end up stereotyping them.

Although they are getting fewer, there are still partnerships in the region operating under the Financier-Partner paradigm. This may be unavoidable due to the economic disparity between the sending and receiving nations. The Asia Pacific region has some of the least developed nations, e.g. Laos, Myanmar, Solomon Islands, Papua New Guinea, etc. In many of these countries, Christians come from the lower economic strata of society. The persistence to operate in the Financier-Partner paradigm could very well be due to a culture of dependency, which has been inculcated over the years. However, we need to understand that local national leaders are not always the "culprit" in perpetuating this culture of dependency. Both the missionary and the local leadership may become very comfortable in this relationship. The missionaries may conveniently continue financial partnership to maintain control and a form of "relevance" in order to remain in the field. Meanwhile, the national churches continue to enjoy material handouts though their economies have grown and they no longer need them.

I would observe that the majority of the countries in the Asia Pacific region currently operate in the Facilitator-Partner paradigm. With a few exceptions, missionaries in the Asia Pacific region seldom do direct "frontline" missions work requiring a one-sided financial arrangement. There is not much "virgin" missions territory left in the

---

[6]The economies in the Asia Pacific region range from some of the poorest nations like Laos, Myanmar, Solomon Islands, North Korea, etc. and also some of the richest nations like Brunei, Japan, Singapore, Hong Kong, South Korea, etc. (https://www.cia.gov/library/publications/the-world-factbook/rankorder/2004rank.html). In this region are also nations that are "closed" to missionary work like Laos, North Korea and Brunei as well as "open" countries like Singapore, Hong Kong, Philippines, etc.

region. Most countries have established national churches with strong local leaderships that can do most, if not all, of the work of missionaries. However, missionaries are still needed to come alongside and help these national churches. For example, at APTS, qualified missionary educators from the West teach in their areas of expertise. With many qualified Asian faculty opting to move to the West, the services of these Western missionary faculty and educators may be needed to keep APTS' academic accreditation. Western missionary faculty also provide an international dimension needed to train leaders to serve in today's globalized world.

Another area where missionaries are working in the Facilitator-Partner paradigm is in international churches and ministries. With globalization and the attractiveness of the Asia Pacific for business investors, there is an exploding mission field of expatriates. The local national leadership may not have the experience to handle this arena. Sometimes, because of legal, cultural and language reasons, it is inconvenient for locals to get involved in international ministries within their own countries. Missionaries come as facilitators to help the national churches reach these expatriates. International churches exist in many of the major cities of the region; most are pioneered and led by missionaries.

It is possible to talk about true collaborative partnerships in countries where the churches are more mature and the national economies are more developed (e.g. Malaysia, Singapore, Korea, and Hong Kong). Western missionary partners in these countries are not seen as financiers or facilitators. Instead, they are considered equal partners, collaborating *interdependently* with the local leadership in synergistic partnerships.

There is also a need for collaborative partnerships among missionaries sent from different countries working together in the same field. When traditional Western missionaries move out of the region, missionaries from the new missions-sending countries like Korea, Philippines, Singapore, and even China begin to exert their influence on the field. However, many of these new non-Western missionaries need mentors with experience and expertise. For example, there is likely as many or more Korean missionaries that serve in the

Philippines, compared to the number of American missionaries. With American missionaries having a longer track record, it would benefit Koreans to be guided by their American colleagues as facilitator-partners, even though Koreans may have no need for American finances. Unfortunately, this has not happened: today, Koreans are repeating the past mistakes of American missionaries. Perhaps, missionary statesmanship and diplomacy could work out the partnerships between old and new missions-sending agencies and countries.

Recent new challenges have arisen in the region as well. Religious fundamentalism and militancy have been on the rise. Terrorist activities have increased in Southern Philippines, Southern Thailand and Indonesia. Meanwhile, a narrow-minded politicized brand of Islam has been encouraged by some extremists in Malaysia. Political upheavals in Myanmar and Thailand are posing challenges while offering opportunities for missionaries at the same time. The Church needs to stand together to face these challenges. The voice of the Church needs to be heard both inside and outside of these countries. Partnerships are still needed.

Beyond Indigenization: Recommendations for Collaborative Contextualization

Contextualization has been a buzzword in missions since the 1970's. It is now often viewed as a development from the earlier idea of indigenization. In indigenization, the goal of the missionary is to help the missions-target church become "self-supporting, self-governing and self-propagating." In contextualization, another layer is added to these "three selves" "self-theologizing." Helping missions-target nations self-theologize is the goal of seminaries like APTS. Indigenization encourages the missions target to *do* things for themselves, but contextualization also encourages them to *think* for themselves. However, theologizing totally from ground zero in the Asia/Pacific context and disengaging or ignoring the theological contributions of the West is like re-inventing the wheel. The ultimate goal of the Collaborator-Partner paradigm is to help leaders from both sending and receiving nations think and work together to accomplish the task of the Great Commission.

APPENDIX 1: Everett McKinneys' Ministry Resumé

Education

MDiv equivalent; DMin studies, Western Conservative Baptist Seminary, 1985 – 1988 (All resident requirements for DMin completed; projects not finished due to family crisis)

MA in Missions, Assemblies of God Theological Seminary, 1976 - 1977

BA in Education (History Major), Cascade College, 1965 - 1967

BA in Bible/Theology, Northwest University, 1958 - 1963

Ministry and Teaching Experience

Bible School Consultant for Asia Pacific Education Office, 1988 - present

Member, Asia Pacific Theological Association, 1988 - present

Member, APTA Teacher Development & Certification Commission, 1988 - present

Teaching/preaching/seminar ministry, 1988 - present

Seminaries: Continental Theological Seminary, Brussels, Belgium; Southern Asia Bible College, Bangalore, India; Evangel Theological Seminary, Kiev, Ukraine

Short-term teaching assignments in Bible schools: Eastern Europe and other Communist or former Communist nations, Southern Asia, Asia Pacific

Non-Resident Faculty, Asia Pacific Theological Seminary (APTS), 1987 - present

Extension Director, Instructor, Chairman of Advisory Council, Director of Development, APTS, 1977 - 1989

President, Instructor, Far East Advanced School of Theology, 1977 - 1984

President, Business Manager, Faculty – Immanuel Bible Institute, 1969 - 1975

Assemblies of God Missionary (USA), 1969 - present

Associate Pastor, Spanaway Assembly of God, 1967 - 1968

Pastor, Skokomish Indian Assembly, 1963 - 1965

Associate Pastor, Arlington Assembly of God, 1962 - 1963

Ministry Team Leader, Northwest University, 1959 - 1962

APPENDIX 2: Evelyn McKinney's Ministry Resume

Education

MDiv equivalent; DMin studies, Western Conservative Baptist Seminary, 1985 - 1988

(All resident requirements for DMin completed; projects not finished due to family crisis)

MA in Missions, Assemblies of God Theological Seminary, 1976 - 1977

Special Studies in Bible, Northwest University, 1975 - 1976

Graduate Studies in Education, Central Washington University, 1961 - 1963 summers

BA in Education and Missions, Seattle Pacific University, 1956 - 1960

Ministry Experience with Husband

Assemblies of God Missionary (USA), 1969 - present

Associate Pastor, Spanaway Assembly of God, 1967 - 1968

Pastor, Skokomish Indian Assembly, 1963 - 1965

Associate Pastor, Arlington Assembly of God, 1962 - 1963

Personal Ministry and Teaching Experience

Teaching/preaching/seminar ministry, 1988 - present

Seminaries: Continental Theological Seminary, Brussels, Belgium; Southern Asia Bible College, Bangalore, India; Evangel Theological Seminary, Kiev, Ukraine

Short-term teaching Assignments in Bible schools: Eastern Europe and other Communist or former Communist nations; Southern Asia, Asia Pacific

Non-Resident Faculty, Asia Pacific Theological Seminary (APTS), 1987 - present

Instructor, APTS, 1977 - 1987 (Interim Academic Dean and Dean of Students for one year of that period)

Instructor, Academic Dean, Immanuel Bible Institute, 1969 - 1975

Public School Teacher, States of Washington and Oregon, USA, 1960 - 1968

CONTRIBUTORS

Dynnice Rosanny D. Engcoy, PhD, is a veteran educator who currently serves as the registrar for Global University in the Philippines.

Kay Fountain, PhD, served as an instructor at the Asia Pacific Theological Seminary in Baguio City, Philippines for over 20 years. She is now retired and living in New Zealand.

Weldyn Houger, DMiss, is a retired Assemblies of God missionary to the Asia Pacific. He and his wife, Barbara, taught in Bible schools in the Asia Pacific Region for over 30 years.

Dave Johnson, DMiss, a missionary in the Asia Pacific Region for over 20 years, is the managing editor of the *Asian Journal of Pentecostal Studies* and the author of two books.

Julie Ma, PhD, a long-term missions educator in both Asia Pacific and Europe, is currently teaching missions at Oral Roberts University in Tulsa, Oklahoma, USA.

Monte Lee Rice, MDiv, has been a missionary in Singapore and Africa for 30 years.

Tham Wan Yee, MTh, is an Assemblies of God missionary from Malaysia and currently serves as the president of the Asia Pacific Theological Seminary in Baguio City, Philippines.

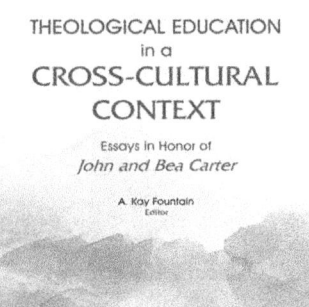
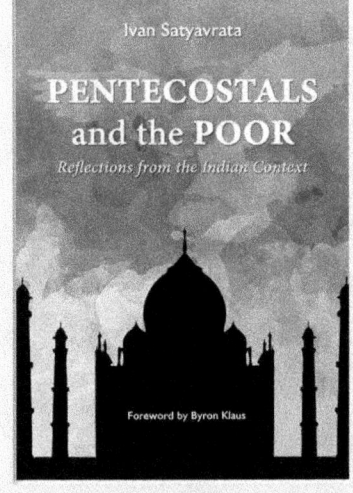

available at www.aptspress.org

available at www.aptspress.org

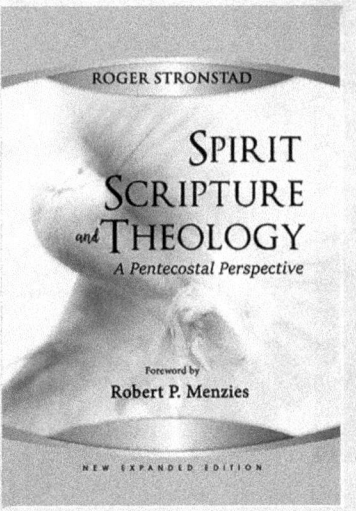

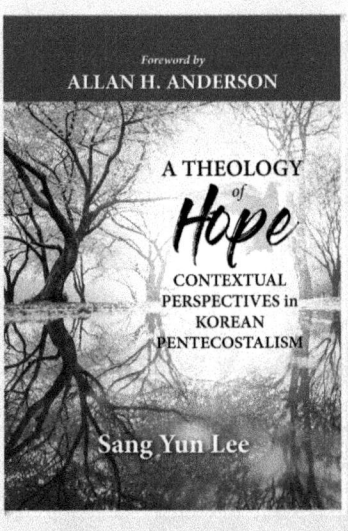

available at www.aptspress.org

www.ingramcontent.com/pod-product-compliance
Lightning Source LLC
Chambersburg PA
CBHW050828160426
43192CB00010B/1943